Women
and
Cocaine

Women
and
COCAINE
Personal Stories
of
Addiction and Recovery

Vicki D. Greenleaf

Lowell House
Los Angeles

Contemporary Books
Chicago

Library of Congress Cataloging-in-Publication Data

Greenleaf, Vicki D.
    Women and Cocaine / Vicki D. Greenleaf.
        p.   cm.
    ISBN 0–929923–11–1
        1. Women—United States—Drug use—Case studies.   2. Cocaine
habit—United States—Case studies.   I. Title.
    HV5824.W6G74   1989
    362.2'982'082—dc20   89-22318
                                                                    CIP

Lowell House
1875 Century Park East
Los Angeles, CA 90067

Publisher: Jack Artenstein
Editor-in-Chief: Janice Gallagher
Marketing Manager: Elizabeth Wood
Design: Gary Hespenheide
Manufactured in the United States of America
10 9 8 7 6 5 4 3 2 1

My most heart-felt gratitude to my husband, my parents, and my grandparents for many years of love, support, and encouragement. And special thanks to Ruth and Janice.

CONTENTS

A PERSONAL NOTE

In 1986 I was a contributing editor to *Playgirl* magazine, writing regularly on women's issues, usually with a feminist bent, on subjects ranging from "Right-Wing Women" to "Sexuality in the South" to "Women and Cocaine."

Certainly "Women and Cocaine" was the most emotional issue I covered. Although it held no personal meaning for me when the story was assigned, I soon became very much involved. The interviews I conducted were both heart-wrenching and aggravating: heart-wrenching for what these women suffered, and aggravating because the prejudice and insensitivity women are frequently exposed to on a day-to-day basis extended even to addiction—something the uninitiated would certainly assume to be the great equalizer, if anything is.

When Lowell House approached me about expanding the article into a book, I saw an opportunity to reach out to a lot of women on a very crucial subject: drugs kill, and cocaine is the most insidious drug of all.

What I had found during my research was that women bear far greater shame in our society for the "sin" of addiction. Those women need to hear that they're not alone, that they're not bad, and that they can regain their lives. They shouldn't have to wear a "Scarlet C" on their brow if they ask for help.

Having worked primarily as a journalist, I discovered this book to be more work than I could ever have imagined. But getting to know the women I interviewed was a very enriching experience. Having gone through so much—and having nearly lost everything—each of them has a unique and generally positive view of life. I admire each and every one of them for what she has overcome and what she has accomplished with her life today. It is my privilege to portray their stories here.

For almost everyone involved it was very difficult to open up old wounds that hadn't hurt in quite a while or new wounds that haven't yet entirely healed, particularly to a virtual stranger. And there was quite a range of emotions, from tears to nervous laughter to embarrassment.

One overriding concern was expressed by each woman who participated: "If I can help someone else get sober or keep her from using in the first place; if I can reach one other person through my own hellish experience, at least I accomplished something through it all."

I felt I had been entrusted with portraying their stories in the spirit in which they were meant to be told, and I nervously awaited the responses when I allowed each woman to read her chapter. When one woman called me, sobbing, my heart began pounding, and I thought, "My God, I've destroyed this woman." But the tears, I was assured, were happy ones, joyous for the comparison of what her life was like then and how wonderful it is today.

Even more important to me was the fact that while I was in college myself, in the late seventies and early eighties, people were still propagating the fallacy that cocaine isn't addictive. Though I was by no means enmeshed in the drug culture, I was lured into enough of a false sense of security to take a snort. Today, considerably older and now considerably wiser, I thank God that cocaine just didn't mix with my body chemistry, even though I experimented with it on several occasions. I absolutely hated the drug. But it could easily have been otherwise. Certainly none of these women expected to become addicts.

What separated me from the women in this book? It wasn't a good upbringing, IQ, education, morals, position, or financial resources— not from what I saw. In fact, it wasn't much at all. And it may well be that just one little gene is what made the difference.

WOMEN AND COCAINE:

WHAT THE EXPERTS HAVE TO SAY ABOUT
THE ISSUES AND PROBLEMS

With more and more women leaving the role of traditional home-maker in recent years, both professionally and socially they have come into contact with daily stresses and temptations that as late as the mid-eighties were generally attributed to men. Consequently, women today comprise one-third to one-half of all substance abusers, including the most recent plague of cocaine addiction. Without a doubt, the experts agree, cocaine has emerged as the illegal drug of choice among women, second only to marijuana.

"I don't think coke has a sexual preference or discrimination, but the cocaine epidemic may be another angle of feminist catch-up time," asserts Michael Meyers, M.D., medical director of Choices at Brotman, a Los Angeles–based drug and alcohol treatment program at the Brotman Medical Center.

"We're talking about a drug that has a lot of positive, reinforcing qualities for women," he continues. "It's not like heroin, which makes you nod out. The woman on cocaine is productive in the office, slim, flirty, loquacious, and gregarious. Cocaine increases sexuality and all these positive things. So you get an external reward, *plus* it makes you feel good inside."

"Addiction is an equal-opportunity disease, and cocaine knows no social, economic, ethnic, or gender boundaries," laments Arnold M.

Washton, Ph.D., executive director of the New York City–based Washton Institute on Addictive Disorders, pioneer of the 1-800-CO-CAINE hotline, and author of several books, including the recent releases *Willpower's Not Enough* and *Cocaine Addiction: Treatment, Recovery, and Relapse Prevention.*

"I think the public finally realizes that anybody can become addicted, irrespective of gender or how educated or uneducated you may be," Washton says. "And the cocaine problem has not stopped spreading. It's a fantasy if we think it's leveling off."

In this chapter, with the help of some of the leading physicians and researchers in the field, we'll look at the statistics that detail cocaine's impact on contemporary women. We'll also examine the reasons why it happens, the special problem of cocaine use during pregnancy, barriers to treatment, the treatment itself, and the question of when it will end. In later chapters we'll also experience the personal stories of addiction and recovery of women across the nation, receive some guidelines for judging whether or not an addiction problem exists in your life, and take an inside look at 12-Step programs like Cocaine Anonymous.

The statistics that surround cocaine abuse are staggering, according to the National Institute on Drug Abuse, the National Narcotic Intelligence Consumers Committee, The Media-Advertising Partnership for a Drug-Free America, and other news sources:

More than 22 million Americans above age 12, or almost 12 percent of the United States population (220 million), have tried cocaine at least once; more than 5 million Americans, or 3 percent of the population, are regular users, and as many as 2 to 3 million users may already be addicted.

The highest percentage of cocaine users, of which one-third to one-half are women, is found in the 18-to-34 age group.

Among high school seniors, more than 17 percent have tried cocaine, and almost 7 percent are already regular users. Nearly a fifth of all children between 9 and 12 years old have been approached to try illegal drugs.

The cost of treating Americans already addicted to cocaine is estimated at between $8 and $30 billion a year.

Hospital emergency-room complaints related to cocaine in the U.S. have risen 700 percent since 1982 and 86 percent in the past year, peaking at nearly 40,000 in 1988, of which 1,582 were fatalities.

As much as 466 tons of cocaine were produced in South American countries in 1987.

It's just not enough to recognize the problem statistically, however. Many of the issues and problems that confront women who are addicted to cocaine, both physically and emotionally, differ dramatically from those faced by men, and only recently have research and treatment begun to focus on these topics. They include a stronger tendency toward depression and considerably lower self-esteem, both a factor in becoming an addict and an impediment to recovery; a perceived lack of empowerment; the crushing stigma of being a female addict; dependency on the male; eating disorders and weight loss; the physiological effects of cocaine on a woman and an increased susceptibility to addiction; a history of sexual, physical, and/or emotional abuse; prostitution (either formal or informal); pregnancy; single parenthood; a lack of financial resources and/or child care that prevents them from seeking treatment; and a lack of treatment programs that address women's issues.

The mechanics of cocaine abuse are relatively simple. Coke is usually bought by the gram at a cost of $80 to $120, depending on the purity and market availability. It is either snorted and absorbed through the mucous membrane in the nose; injected; or, after chemical conversion to a purified form known as freebase, or "crack," smoked. A dose, or a "line," as it's called, is at least 20 to 30 milligrams, although most addicts administer larger amounts.

Specific physical effects of a single dose of cocaine last 30 to 60 minutes and include constricted peripheral blood vessels; dilated pupils; increased body temperature, heart rate, and blood pressure; euphoria; hyperstimulation; reduced fatigue; and a perceived increase in mental clarity.

Telltale signs of cocaine use include forgetfulness; weight loss; loss of interest in physical appearance, friends, sports, hobbies, and other non-cocaine-related activities; chronic runny nose; frequent upper-respiratory infections; hyperactivity; repeated compulsive acts such as tapping of fingers or playing with hair; sleeplessness; mood swings characterized by impatience, nervousness, belligerence and depression; irresponsibility; and newfound financial woes.

Unlike alcohol, which is not detrimental when used in moderation, just one experience with cocaine can be harmful, even life threatening, depending on the person. There is clear evidence that cocaine users are at considerably higher risk to suffer heart attacks, seizures, strokes, or cerebral hemorrhages. They may also have a greater incidence of high blood pressure, irregular heartbeat, respiratory infection, paranoia, and depression.

Additionally, cocaine, particularly when smoked, or freebased, is one of the most addictive drugs known.

Testifies Monica, a Miami high school teacher interviewed in this book, "I loved it! It did for me what I couldn't do for myself."

"From the first day I began a pretty heavy love affair with cocaine," seconds Cathy, a Los Angeles teenager who was also interviewed. "I loved the drug and just buried my face in it."

Since widespread recreational use of cocaine is a relatively new phenomenon—it first became readily available only in the late seventies—its long-term effects are not yet fully known. However, many experts are beginning to find evidence of far-reaching damage.

"Most of the memory disorders and other kinds of acute mental problems cocaine causes tend to clear up," relates Carol Atkinson, Ph.D., director of the cocaine clinic of the Addiction Research and Treatment Services at the University of Colorado School of Medicine. "But I have heard of cocaine psychosis that took a long time and may have been permanent. We also suspect there may be more paranoid disorders in the future among people who are using cocaine now."

Experts are all quick to point out, however, that almost without exception a cocaine user is also addicted to other substances, primarily alcohol or narcotics, which are used to "take the edge off," or quiet the nervous side effects, of cocaine. And some of the detrimental effects on health may be attributed to those dual addictions.

"I think you have to appreciate that people don't use cocaine alone," explains Blanche Frank, Ph.D., chief of epidemiology of the Bureau of Research and Evaluation for the New York State Division of Substance Abuse Services. "They use it in combination with alcohol and other drugs. I don't know a 'pure' cocaine user. And because people are using many drugs together, including tobacco, it's very hard to separate the causes from the effects. But even if you talk about doing cocaine alone, you're really running a major risk."

Although experts differentiate between abusers, or "chippers," and addicts, it's a thin line, and most stress that a woman cannot judge her predisposition to addiction unless she takes the risk of exposing herself to the possibility.

"An abuser will take a drug to a point where she puts herself at risk or even suffers some consequence. But at some point she says it's not worth it, pulls back from it, and doesn't have trouble doing that," differentiates Washton. "The addict experiences consequences from drug use, and then she uses even more.

"Cocaine is a drug that's short-acting and, consequently, it's a drug that people feel they can control. But they're playing with fire."

THE REASONS WHY
Cocaine is the perfect ladylike drug. There are no unsightly needle marks, no smells, no unsavory hanging around bars. Also, it's slimming, it's sensual, you're not in a stupor, you don't slur your words, and you can carry it around in your cosmetic case just like a lipstick. Coke has also become a sort of modern version of flowers and candy. According to *MS.* magazine, some 87 percent of all the women in a recent survey of one cocaine hotline had been introduced to the drug by men, and 65 percent continued to receive cocaine as "gifts."

For women, who are raised with much stricter social mores and guidelines than men, it may be an especially pleasing drug due to its ability to banish inhibitions. But more importantly, experts today are beginning to understand that addicts seem to be attempting to "self-medicate," a phenomenon considered to be especially true among women. This counters years of study in which researchers attributed drug use to pleasure-seeking or self-destructive behavior, particularly among men who more typically display antisocial behavior.

"I can't give you a portrait of someone likely to become an addict," explains Edward Khantzian, M.D., principal psychiatrist for substance-abuse disorders at Cambridge Hospital and an associate professor of psychiatry at the Harvard Medical School. "But, if a woman is anxious or depressed, perhaps not even overtly; if she's isolated, cut off from other people, or in an overly dependent relationship; if she has poor self-esteem and doesn't take good care of herself; or if she's been exposed to major trauma, disappointment, or dysfunctional living, then I think she's more apt to experiment with and get hooked on drugs."

Becoming Somebody: The Low Self-Esteem Issue

One new theory claims that addicts don't choose their drug haphazardly but through a process of elimination, settling on the substance that best addresses their particular "needs." Some experts claim that more than 90 percent of all addicts, particularly women (who characteristically tend to be more expressive emotionally than men), have some underlying psychiatric or emotional disorder, most notably depression and/or low self-esteem. Cocaine has qualities that are especially reinforcing in those situations.

Khantzian, who authored a 1985 cover story in the *American Journal of Psychiatry* titled "The Self-Medication Hypothesis of Addictive Disorders: Focus on Heroin and Cocaine Dependence," has done studies which revealed that cocaine appeals to people who are feeling either depressively low or hyperactively high, making it particularly insidious because it is responsive to a wide range of ills.

According to Khantzian, "Men live out their psychological problems of distress and suffering through action and ambition. They may be covertly depressed, but they don't have the overt symptoms of low energy, gloomy outlook, poor appetite, and sleep disturbances, although they may have a single symptom. Women seem to feel free to have sad, depressed feelings and a gloomy outlook."

Consequently, cocaine's chemical effect on the brain and its resulting feeling of euphoria, at least initially, would tend to earmark it for women. Its ability to bolster self-confidence and provide a sense of empowerment may also endear it to disenfranchised groups such as women.

"If you look at the properties of cocaine and what people say happens to them under the influence, they're trying to feel better and more powerful. People say they feel almost God-like, sexually potent, and just potent as a human being in general," explains Kevin McEneaney, senior vice-president and director of clinical services for the New York–based Phoenix House, the nation's largest private inpatient addiction program, which acted as counsel to the Reagan administration's antidrug crusade. "If these people need that so badly, I think we would do better to look at the people rather than the drug. What is it in this society and the experience of living in this culture that makes them not feel good about themselves no matter what they do? What is it that makes them need something that actually tells them they're doing better than they really are? Because that's a property of cocaine."

Traditionally, women have been socialized to nurture men and their needs, they are frequently not financially or emotionally independent, and they usually bear primary responsibility for the home and children whether they work or not. Consequently, most women suffer from much lower self-esteem than their male counterparts. They feel ineffectual, unable to change their situation; so they look for an external solution.

"Men are really in a different situation," proposes Gloria Weissman, deputy branch chief of the Community Research Branch Division of Applied Research of the National Institute on Drug Abuse (NIDA). "Male self-esteem is higher, or they at least perceive themselves as having power—which in fact they usually do, at least in their domestic lives. Most addicted women are in a situation where they have very little power and no sense of being able to change things. What may begin as a coping mechanism to deal with a psychological problem then becomes dysfunctional itself. You have to find some way to get that woman off the drug, but you also have to deal with the underlying problem. They have to be able to cope with their lives."

"Men take their anger out externally, on their secretary or wife or the dog. Women internalize it. That's how some people define depression, as internalizing your anger," submits Michael Tinken, vice-president of community relations for Lifeline cocaine dependency treatment center in Chicago. "We do see more depression and passivity in women. They're just not dealing with their problems, and they're not real assertive about how they feel about things. That's something that needs to be worked on in treatment, how to say no to somebody and feel comfortable with it. They obviously weren't comfortable enough to say no to drugs."

The Pressure Cooker: Women at Work
Corporate America has become increasingly dependent on women, who now account for 40 percent of all managers, compared to less than 20 percent in 1970.

"Women have achieved considerable status in recent years, and they've worked hard for it," according to Boston-area psychologist

John Barry, Ph.D. "Usually they've put in more time, effort, and energy to achieve equivalent status to men. As a consequence, to keep up that kind of pace, some of them are wide open for an addiction. They pay quite a price ascending the corporate ladder."

Khantzian agrees: "I believe that the marketplace requires energy, a sense of power, and fuel to bring all those standards to fruition. I don't think we should be at all surprised that the kinds of things that drive men in the marketplace—and leave them susceptible to a whole range of disorders—are now affecting women more and more."

"People who are upwardly mobile, who are coming into their own—which women are—find cocaine to be very attractive," says Elaine Johnson, Ph.D., director of the federal Office for Substance Abuse Prevention in Rockville, Maryland. "It's the drug of choice. Whereas other drugs dull their senses, cocaine makes them feel like they're on top of the situation and gives them a feeling of performance enhancement."

"We've seen more women get into cocaine because more women are becoming type-A personalities," confirms Myra Byanka, founder and director of The Southwestern Behavioral Institute, a Dallas-based consultancy firm that oversees recovery-program start-ups. "Competitive women are living a pseudomasculine existence. The way we're supposed to feel good about ourselves is to act like men. Females now tend to develop the same kind of stress reactions as males. Consequently, we're dying of heart attacks and developing drug dependencies."

Not only are more women coming into contact with the daily pressures of the work place, but they continue to maintain primary responsibility for the home and children. According to a recent *USA Today* interview with psychologist Lori Temple of the University of Nevada, Las Vegas, working wives and mothers most likely carry up to two-thirds of the domestic work load as well.

"Cocaine is a stimulant, and it really gets you going," relates Frank. "For a lot of women it's the energy that attracts them. We've had women tell us they couldn't clean the house if they didn't have a snort."

"I just spoke to a businesswoman, married with three kids, who is addicted to crack," contributes Delores Morgan, M.D., former director of addictionology services at Mount Sinai Medical Center in Miami. "She works real hard, she's tired, then she has to come home and take care of the kids and the house. So she's stressed out, and a male friend comes along and says, 'Hey, I know something that can help you.' Not only did it help pick her up, but it also helped her lose a little weight. In no time at all, she became an addict."

Perhaps Yvonne, a recovering addict interviewed for this book who is an emergency-room physician in a major hospital and also the director of a prominent addiction-recovery program in the New England area, tells it best:

"I was trying to run a house, take care of my children, and work 80 hours a week. I demanded things from my husband that he didn't want to give, like time with the kids or helping around the house. Even when my ankle was in a cast once for six weeks, I still had to do laundry, cook food, go to work, etc. If I were the man in this relationship, I would have been pampered. It was horrible, and I used cocaine to cope with it.

"Men are supposed to go out and build monuments and bring home dinner. Women are supposed to be home sitting on the eggs. I don't think that's bad—*somebody* in society has to take on the role of caretaker—but it doesn't leave a hell of a lot of room to get sick."

Am I at Greater Risk Than He Is? The Addictive Personality

There is considerable debate in the addiction-rehabilitation field as to whether or not there are genetic markers that predispose someone to addiction from birth, that destine them to become substance abusers from their first drink, puff, or snort.

"Biochemical studies suggest that drug users may have a different brain chemistry than people who aren't users," asserts NIDA's Weissman, "and basically they're using drugs to become—quote, unquote—normal. But we don't know what those mechanisms are."

Taking it even one step further, many experts—although not all of them, by any means—stand by the addictive-personality theory and further assert that it's more common among women and that it may have a physiological root as deep as the social reasons. A few bold clinicians even venture that on the average, women often progress from recreational use of cocaine to addiction much more quickly than do men.

Kathleen Kinney is chairwoman of the North American Women's Commission on Alcohol and Drugs and also the executive director of the Lake Area Recovery Center, an intensive inpatient program in Ohio. "People become far more critical of women a lot sooner than they do of men," she explains. "Women start to feel guilty, and then they use more to hide the shame, and it just feeds itself. But I really feel strongly that there's a physiological reason as well."

The University of Colorado's Atkinson confirms this theory: "The evidence is that addiction tends to hit women harder physically than men."

In fact, a recent study on the neuropsychology of sex differences, presented by specialists in the discipline at a 1989 gathering of the New York Academy of Sciences, found subtle variances in the anatomical structures of the brains of men and women that included the shape and size of various parts and sectors. Though the study did not encompass the possible effects on predisposition to addiction, it did indicate that women may react very differently than men to a variety of stimuli.

There is also some speculation that female reaction to intoxicating substances may vary in relationship to changing hormone levels related to menstruation. Although the evidence is unclear and inconsistent, according to the National Institute on Drug Abuse, studies done in 1976 show that women develop higher blood-alcohol levels at the premenstrum compared to identical levels of consumption during menstruation or at other times of the month. And some patients being treated for alcoholism reported that they tended to drink most heavily to relieve premenstrual tensions and ailments.

"It's also possible that the effect of cocaine on the brain—the increased release of dopamine, norepinephrine, seratonin, all of those chemicals—are depleted earlier in women," suggests Lifeline's Tinken. "They may have less of a storage from the start; therefore, their cravings would be stronger, making the progression occur faster."

"We also know that women have more body fat than men do, and cocaine can be stored in the fat," adds physician Meyers. "But women have less water. Since cocaine is distributed only in body water, a woman has less fluid in which to dilute it than does a similarly sized man. Consequently, women have higher concentrations of cocaine in their bloodstream and may therefore become toxic more quickly."

While those theories remain in debate, experts do agree that social environment (exposure to drug use), whether it's parental use in front of a child or peer use during adulthood, has a strong influence on whether or not someone begins to abuse drugs and/or alcohol. Weissman, whose work has specifically dealt with the treatment of women and female adolescents, feels those early family patterns may affect women more deeply than men, though it can be disastrous to both.

"We need to look at family patterns and drug use on the part of the mother and father. We know that one thing that produces drug abuse in men and women is a dysfunctional family in childhood. But I think the effect of those families is very often more toxic and problematic for female children than it is for males because girls are more enmeshed in the family. From infancy, people tend to see a male child as more independent. There's a much stronger identification with a female child and what goes on in the family. I think a lot of that tends to come out in drug use later on."

Additionally, while physical and emotional abuse are damaging enough, female children—not their male siblings—are the ones almost exclusively burdened with sexual abuse. "You also see a high percentage of women addicts who were sexually abused during their childhood and adolescence," Tinken says. "They blame themselves for it in some distorted way and have somehow been numbing or escaping those feelings with drugs."

Confirms Washton, "Being the victim of chemically dependent or sexually abusive parents all but guarantees that a woman will become an addict."

"We see a generational trend, the influence of parents who were abusers as well; we see an environmental trend, the influence of mates and friends; and we see a biological trend, or hereditary predisposition to addiction," Kinney asserts. "The other day I spoke to someone in treatment who is a fourth-generation addict."

But, as Meyers insists, "You don't have to be from the barrio or have a horrible family situation. This is an equal-opportunity destroyer. And they're not bad or weak-willed people. They're good people, and it's a disease."

Female children are also socialized much more than their male siblings to expect to take drugs. Women are larger consumers of over-the-counter medicines and are given prescriptions by physicians for psychoactive drugs, such as tranquilizers, much more frequently than men, although men complain of the same symptoms.

"Women are expected to be less self-reliant, more dependent on others, and takers of drugs," proclaims Sheila Blume, M.D., medical director of the Alcoholism, Chemical Dependency, and Compulsive Gambling Program at South Oaks Hospital in New York, who specializes in female addiction. "Women are twice as likely to get a prescription from a doctor, which is sad but true, and I think in this culture both sexes are socialized into that expectation. There have been studies in which people of both sexes were sent to a physician with the same complaint, and men got one kind of treatment and women got another. One of the experiments was for weight control. The men were prescribed diet and exercise, and the women received diet pills."

I Can Feel This Good and Lose Weight Too?

Another newly noted phenomenon among female cocaine abusers is the distinct relationship to such eating disorders as anorexia and bulimia. Weight loss may not be the reason these women first try cocaine, but it is a welcome side effect.

"The bottom line is that this is a thin-is-beautiful society. But the images the media portray are crazy in my opinion. The person you think you should be is a freak," expounds William Rader, M.D., founder and clinical director of The Rader Institute, Los Angeles, a leading treatment program for eating disorders, a field he helped pioneer, in a 1986 interview.

"Weight loss is not why most women initially take cocaine, but they find it's a side effect and get caught in a trap. As with any other addiction, the person who is hooked desperately searches for some kind of rationalization, for some kind of denial and this excuse presents itself right up front. We frequently see the dual problems of cocaine and bulimia. Cocaine gives you that euphoria and suppresses your appetite. In the beginning it seems like the magic cure."

Blume, who has specialized in female addiction, primarily alcohol, for 27 years, concurs about the link between women, cocaine, and weight loss. "Women do like cocaine for different reasons than men," she says. "I seldom see a male who even thinks about the caloric content of the drug he's using. But women are concerned about their looks and weight and keeping up with the latest fashion. They begin drinking and like what drinking does for them. But then they start to worry about calories and weight. Alcohol has quite a high calorie count.

"Very commonly we see young women addicted to cocaine who have symptoms of anorexia or bulimia, although it may not be in a clinically acute stage. I think they take the drug primarily for the high, but the side effect of appetite control makes the drug even more attractive."

"A small percentage may seek out cocaine as an appetite suppressant," concedes Meyers, who recently expanded his addiction program at Brotman to include eating disorders. "But that's almost irrelevant when you look at how quickly the seductive psychoactive nature of the drug takes hold. And it's almost like asking, 'What came first, the chicken or the egg?' We treat first whichever malady is most life threatening, the eating disorder or the addiction."

The connection may also be, some experts point out, the common personality traits shared by both addicts and victims of eating disorders.

Claims Tinken, "There's a lot of debate in the field about whether or not an addictive personality exists, but personality studies on people in our treatment programs did find that most addicts are perfectionists. They're very compulsive in a number of ways, including the use of cocaine, and may also get into other compulsive behavior such as under- or overeating. They're into achievement, and they want to achieve the 'perfect' body. Whatever they do, whether it's cleaning the house, working on a project, or doing a drug, they overdo."

Most experts emphasize that if both the addiction and the compulsion problems are not treated, rehabilitation will be a hopeless feat. Kelly, a recovering anorexic/bulimic/addict interviewed in this book and who now works at The Rader Institute, suffered a recovery relapse before she finally kicked an addiction to cocaine stemming from nontreatment of her bulimia.

"I didn't know what an eating disorder was then," she explains, "but I did believe that if I didn't have cocaine, I'd get fat. I admitted I was an alcoholic, but I didn't tell anybody about the drugs. The day I got out of rehabilitation for the first time, I took speed."

The Ultimate Aphrodisiac

Another outstanding characteristic of cocaine is its aphrodisiac properties, for which men in particular seek it out. In fact, most women are introduced to cocaine by a date or other male companion.

"Cocaine is a euphoria-producing drug that people often describe as similar to 100 orgasms," says Dr. Morgan. "Initially it is a very sexually oriented drug. But as time goes on and people become more involved with cocaine, they forget the sex and get attached to the drug itself."

Even the act of ingesting cocaine is sexual in a ritualistic way to which using other drugs can't compare—the tapping of a razor edge against mirrored glass to smooth powder, the loving motion of carefully cutting linear portions, the gentle and precise rolling of a currency note. To many addicts it's chemical foreplay.

"Cocaine is a fabulous drug in a way the others aren't," details Dr. Rader. "It's a major social event. You pour alcohol, roll a joint, and pop a pill; but doing cocaine is a very sensual, intimate ritual. You get into a very tight space, like a bathroom, and perform certain mechanics. It's hip, it's bad, it's illegal and extravagant, and you're sharing it. It's a very trusting thing."

Additionally, says The Southwestern Behavioral Institute's Byanka, "Coke acts as a permitter. People find themselves in a state of consciousness that allows them to do sexual things they wouldn't normally do. Sadly, a lot of women ages 14 to 35 are prostituting themselves, trading off sexual favors for cocaine."

Rader concurs but points out a fallacy in that "cocaine is not a true aphrodisiac. It may allow you to participate in something you wouldn't normally do because of anxiety, but it really just plays with what's going on in your mind. It may make you sexual, but it can make you asexual; it may make you impotent, or give you a sustained erection. But it's certainly more socially acceptable to attribute your cocaine use to its enhancing your sex life than it is to admit you are a drug addict."

In actuality, however, it is only socially acceptable for a man to participate in increased or uninhibited sexual behavior. Women have been socialized to feel guilt for such uninhibited behavior, whereas men most frequently view such acts as trophies or accomplishments.

"In the drug world," relates Byanka, "a male cocaine addict is sort of a flashy, interesting character, but a female cocaine addict is always a slut, a coke whore. She's done something bad sexually. It may not be true, but that's the way men look at women who use cocaine."

Explains Tinken, "Most women may not define themselves as working prostitutes, but there's a continuum; you can exchange sex for all sorts of things. What keeps coming up over and over again for most of these women is that their drug use and their sexual lives are so closely intertwined that you can't talk about one without talking about the other. Whether their drug abuse led them into prostitution, whether they're trading sex for drugs, or whether the drug was just used in a sexual setting, there tends to be a very, very close connection there. The drugs may even be a substitute for satisfaction of sexual urges. Cocaine is a very sexual drug."

"That's been the terrible choice women have made in order to get the drug," laments Frank. "It's an unfortunate fact that once you're under the influence of cocaine, you'll do anything to get the drug; you just don't care. You do things you never thought you could possibly bring yourself to do."

A SPECIAL PROBLEM: COCAINE USE DURING PREGNANCY

"The problem of cocaine abuse *is* increasing within the female population, but certainly we had no idea that middle-class women who are pregnant are using cocaine to the extent that they are," asserts Johnson of the federal office for Substance Abuse Prevention, which co-sponsored a survey of hospital obstetrics programs with Ira Chasnoff, M.D., assistant professor of pediatrics and psychiatry and director of the Perinatal Center for Chemical Dependence at Northwestern University Medical School in Chicago. The survey found that at least 11 percent of 155,000 women in 36 U.S. hospitals had been exposed to cocaine or other illegal drugs. That data, experts say, suggests that 375,000 newborns, or one in 10 births, each year face the possibility of health damage from their mother's drug abuse.

"There are women who wouldn't smoke or drink while they were pregnant but who couldn't stay away from cocaine," says Chasnoff, who even recalls one woman receiving a gift of cocaine from her husband to celebrate the announcement of her pregnancy. Most experts agree that it's not lack of education that allows these mothers to continue using drugs throughout pregnancy, it's simply a testimony to the powerful lure of cocaine, one of the most highly addictive drugs around.

"I think that every woman on the street knows that the use of cocaine is bad for her baby," shrugs Stephen Ambrose, clinical psychologist and director of the New Beginnings Project at the Children's Institute in Los Angeles, which has an inpatient program for 47 drug-addicted babies and an outpatient counseling program for parents learning to cope. "But they can't stop. They use, they feel terribly guilty about it, and it's a vicious cycle. If you're a drug addict, the way you're going to deal with the negative effects of guilt is to get high again and try to escape it.

"Also, if a woman admits she has a drug problem while she's pregnant, that will result in the loss of her baby. It's related to the whole issue of when does a fetus become a baby? So it's really a denial process. But once the baby's born, these women are slapped in the face with reality. They have this baby twitching in front of them and going through withdrawal. It's very traumatic."

Cocaine use by an expectant mother triggers spasms in the baby's blood vessels, and the vital flow of oxygen and nutrients can be severely restricted for long periods. According to experts, even one-time use can be damaging to a fetus.

Among women who use cocaine there is a higher incidence of spontaneous abortion. If a baby is carried to term, cocaine-using women tend to have a higher incidence of premature delivery and complications. Also, fetal growth may be retarded, including impairment of head and brain size (which may indicate a lower IQ); birth weight is lower; the babies score lower on the Apgar scale, which measures the general health of a newborn; strokes and seizures may have occurred *in utero*; and there may be malformations of the kidneys, genitals, intestines, and spinal cord.

Laments Johnson, "We're producing a new generation of innocent addicts."

An infant who is born addicted to cocaine will suffer such symptoms of withdrawal as the jitters, inconsolable crying, tense or lax muscle tone, concentration problems, and emotional detachment. Additionally, the risk of Sudden Infant Death Syndrome among children who are now referred to as "drug babies" is five to ten times more common than in the general population, experts say.

What may be even more harmful to a developing fetus than the actual drug exposure is lack of adequate nutrition and prenatal care. Many mothers do not obtain obstetric care because they are afraid of being identified as an addict. Often they are so addicted to cocaine, a known appetite suppressant and stimulant, that they do not eat or sleep properly. In addition, the long-range effects of cocaine abuse on apparently healthy newborns as they approach adolescence are now coming into question.

"People are beginning to be concerned about learning disabilities in later life," states Ambrose. "They are not major neurological dysfunctions, but they are significant. There are some kids who are now being labeled hyperactive or as having attention-deficit disorder who are that way due to prenatal drug exposure. I assume there are many undiagnosed drug babies who are later given those labels. These children have delays in coordination skills and language development, as well as difficulties in forming emotional attachments."

Some studies suggest, however, that most drug babies will grow up at normal or near-normal levels and that emotional problems and other difficulties are more likely linked to growing up in an unstable home environment than to fetal drug exposure.

BARRIERS TO TREATMENT
Many of the prejudicial issues that addicted women face in today's society act as actual deterrents to their seeking help. Women may be fearful of the harsh stigma attached to a female cocaine addict, and so they are in deep denial; they may have a husband or boyfriend who is either discouraging them verbally or simply refusing to help finance rehabilitation; or they may be afraid their admission of drug use will result in custodial loss of their children.

Who, Me?
Many experts describe addiction as the only disease that symptomatically tells its victim she or he has no problem. Additionally, cocaine addicts, unlike other substance abusers, are highly "functional," at least initially. Plus, their drug use doesn't produce the obvious signs of intoxification associated with alcohol, marijuana, opiates, or other drugs.

"Detection of cocaine abuse is often difficult to discern," admits Susan Thompson, a former executive in a Los Angeles–based company that sets up employee-assistance programs in large corporations and small companies to reach workers with dependency problems. "You can do cocaine at work, and nobody is going to know. They're not going to see track marks or smell it on your breath. But where it may take an alcoholic 25 years to destroy everything—family, job, and credit—it can happen as quickly as 90 days with cocaine."

Many addicts use their ability to function and their position in the community or job market to justify their increasingly erratic behavior. A woman can find many other reasons to rationalize her behavior as well.

According to Marva Miller, formerly an addiction counselor with the now-defunct Beverly Glen Hospital cocaine program in Los Angeles, "Women are more difficult to treat because their denial system is more sophisticated. They justify their addiction through their jobs or the prestige they hold in the community or their families. They can't be cocaine addicts, because they make too much money or because they're married."

"It's like having a brain tumor—because your thinking is grossly distorted," adds Rader. "Cocaine addicts are not going to reach out for help, because they think the problem is with you, not them. You can't expect these addicts to get help, because they have no idea they need it."

Insists Frank, "These people aren't stereotypical drug addicts. The kind of thing that was previously a red flag for drug use just doesn't exist anymore. I think that shows the strength of the drug."

"That's the insanity," adds Morgan. "We see it all the time. Someone comes in who takes vitamins, jogs, and uses cocaine. She's got a hole in her nose, but she wants to know if she can exercise to keep up her health. We just don't admit we have a problem."

"I don't know if they're rationalizing or if they say, 'Well, this is my coping strategy, so I'll do it and compensate for it in some other way—by eating right or working out,'" explains Johnson. "They think, 'That won't happen to me.' And that's just not true with the drug issue. It's happening in so many families and so many communities."

But it may not only be the addict herself who is in denial. Spouses, boyfriends, family members, friends, and co-workers are not likely to recognize the symptoms of addiction until the later stages. "It's amazing the kind of rationalizations and excuses we make for people when we want to," Frank says incredulously.

Johnson concurs with that statement. "In the initial stages of cocaine addiction, addicts *are* highly functional. There may be some symptoms, but most people would never guess the problem was drugs. If you're not looking for something, you just keep attributing it to some other cause. That's denial too."

Denial, most experts admit, is deeply rooted in the inescapable stigma associated with either being—or being associated with—a female cocaine addict.

The Scarlet C

Once a woman overcomes her denial and all the other barriers to obtaining treatment, she is faced with yet another difficulty, one so crushing that it could dissolve her resolve to attain sobriety: social unacceptability. "Regardless of what we'd like to think about the women's movement, certain behavior, like drug behavior—getting drunk, smoking dope, or using coke—is more acceptable if you're a man. That's just how it is," says Byanka bluntly.

"I think people generally see women addicts as people not to be respected, as women who have overstepped their boundaries," Washton agrees. "With men it's just a natural extension of the male lifestyle.

"Part of the reason women don't come in more for treatment is the social stigma. It's okay for men to be heavy drinkers or partiers or drug users, but such behavior isn't feminine or ladylike. Women are the societal gatekeepers, so to speak. They're supposed to be mothers. They represent what's supposed to be right and good."

"It's a pretty chauvinistic observation," Meyers admits, "but it's that double standard one more time. A woman who uses is automatically branded with the connotation of being a coke whore, with selling her body for the drug."

While neither male nor female is proud to admit to being an addict, there is no way to deny that women are burdened with an extremely harsh stigma. There's the attitude that a woman of such low moral fiber deserves her plight and, even if sober now, should not be allowed to resume her rightful place in society.

"We have very strong negative feelings about women who drink or use drugs," Blume sighs. "Women are expected to pass morality down from one generation to the next. So women who drink are more stigmatized. And there's the idea that dates back to the ancient Romans that alcohol makes women promiscuous. I would say that crosses over to cocaine use.

"There was a study by the University of Georgia in Athens, where they gave out a scenario of an actual rape case to 200 college students," she continues. "They were presented with four different versions. In one the man was drunk, and the woman who was raped was sober. In another the woman was drunk, and the man was sober. In another both of them were drunk, and in the last neither was drinking. Both male and female respondents rated the man who was drunk less responsible for what happened and the woman who was drunk more responsible, even in the case where they were both drinking. So women who drink are considered acceptable targets—they get what they asked for."

Even among addicts themselves there exists a caste system. A male addict will look down on a woman in the same situation as himself. "There are social classes within the using population, not only according to sex, but also what type of drug you use," Chasnoff explains.

To further complicate matters, men are commonly humiliated by their mate's or their daughter's behavior, and so they are much less likely to stand by a wife or girlfriend who has an addiction than the reverse situation. The members of family support groups are primarily female.

"No matter what they portray on *Cagney and Lacey*," laments Byanka, "there is still relatively little support in terms of self-esteem for women. They have to live with the day-to-day prejudices. Men are embarrassed by their wives, and that's the real heart of the problem. A man will just divorce a woman with an addiction problem. Why do you think Al-Anon is full of women? Because it stands by its members.

"We're supposed to be the caretakers," she continues. "Men don't want to take care of us. They'll pay for things because that's what they think they're supposed to do. But when we get sick or have a headache or can't perform, they get angry. You see a lot of anger in the husbands and fathers of drug-addicted females. And it's acculturated."

Adds Weissman, "Women will urge men to get help, but very few women are urged into treatment by their male partners. Their mates may not be willing to lose their services in the home. What's he going to do with the children? There are tremendous barriers."

But He Doesn't Want Me to Go

Women are often dependent on men both to maintain their drug addiction and to escape it. Most frequently, women are enmeshed in relationships with men who are also drug abusers. Such husbands or boyfriends may not be encouraging to a woman in her quest for sobriety. He may even be, whether it's intentional or not, emotionally sabotaging her.

Most clinicians agree that before they can rehabilitate a woman to long-term recovery, they frequently need to remove her from the emotional instability common in drug-derivative relationships; a living situation that may have been her cause to attempt "self-medication" to begin with. Many female abusers are addicted to men for gratification as much as they are to cocaine. "In the same way that people look to drugs to 'fix' them, women also use men for the same purposes, to feel good about themselves," Lifelines' Meyers asserts. "They're addicted to people just as they are to drugs. Although the dynamic of an addict who is co-dependent cuts across sexual boundaries, I think it's more dramatic in a woman because of financial setup and social stigma."

Adds Blume, "Women also tend to be underemployed or in lower-paying jobs without health coverage, making them even more dependent on men. It's really tough."

According to the North American Women's Commission on Alcohol and Drugs' Kathleen Kinney, "Dependency on a male is a big issue for female cocaine addicts. They need to have an understanding of how you can have a healthy relationship with a man and not be totally dependent for all things. They have to be able to achieve some self-esteem and believe that they can function in a healthy way without being dependent on a man for all gratification, whether it's drug-related or not."

"I was absolutely dependent on the man in my life—emotionally, financially, and for drugs. I turned all decisions over to him. Whatever he wanted, was what I wanted," confesses Sarah, a criminal defense lawyer and an eighties-style woman whose discussion of her addiction in this book breaks several popular preconceptions. Her live-in boyfriend, she says, introduced her to cocaine. To escape both influences, she was forced to sneak away in the middle of the night. Only then was she able to seek treatment.

But it is not only romantic relationships that take on distorted dynamics for women. The same pattern of interaction extends to friends and co-workers, who also frequently go out of their way to cover up for her. This system of networking may allow a woman to escape detection of her addiction longer and keep her from obtaining the help she so desperately needs.

"Women get insulated in their drug abuse. Through resources of their own they often have someone to take care of them, and they've been able to mask the problem. They're able to prolong their addictions because of the kinds of relationships they get themselves into," says Phoenix House's McEneaney. "It's a systematic problem, and it goes back 20 years. Men go out and steal and rob and aggressive stuff like that. And while we're now beginning to see the same acts from women, they have other ways of maintaining a drug-addicted lifestyle, regardless of whether they're lower, middle, or upper class. Drug-abusing women develop very strange relationships. People take care of them in return for sex and other favors, and it's a very symbiotic, sick relationship, whether it's on the job or at home. That can go on for months and months."

Diana, a financial loan analyst in Los Angeles who was interviewed for this book, typified this behavior. "I made a lot of serious mistakes at work. I was covering up, and my manager also covered for me. She saved my ass many, many times. If I couldn't make it to work, it was okay with her. She thought of me as a daughter. Being the conniving and manipulative drug addict that I was, I was able to crawl under their skins. I made them sort of love me so that they wouldn't fire me. But they weren't doing me any favors. If they had fired me, I probably would have hit my bottom earlier and gone for help."

Experts stress that rather than "enabling," or assisting an addict, friends, family, and co-workers should risk her anger and confront her, no matter how strong her denial.

Mothers on Cocaine: "I Don't Want to Lose My Baby"

Substance abuse certainly bears influence on the climbing rate of child abuse, as so recently brought to national attention by the 1988–89 trial of freebase addicts Joel Steinberg and Hedda Nussbaum in New York City, both charged with the death of their illegally adopted daughter, Lisa.

"If you have a baby who cries inconsolably and has difficulty in forming attachments and a drug-involved mother who is consequently irritable and volatile, it's a dangerous combination," suggests the New Beginnings Project's Ambrose. "Sometimes the cocaine lifestyle can be very violent."

It's unfair, however, to stereotypically assume that *all* cocaine addicts are guilty of child abuse, and yet in many states a woman's mere identification as a drug user—whether her children have been properly cared for or not—is grounds for loss of custody. Most experts view this as an impediment for women to get help for their addiction.

"There are tremendous barriers that men don't face," says Blume. "For example, being a single parent is a woman's role in our society. And a young woman with children is a very common role that's often affected by drugs and alcohol. It's very hard for such a woman to get into a treatment program without adequate child care. And if she did get help, chances are she would be charged with child neglect and lose custody of her children.

"In many states the definition of child neglect includes being habituated to alcohol or drugs or being an immoderate user, as the statutes put it. A smart husband, in a divorce or custody case, could use that. I'm very proud of the fact that in New York I helped change the law to read that if a parent is participating in a program of drug rehabilitation, that presumption of neglect doesn't hold. There now has to be clear evidence of neglect or abuse. So now instead of being a barrier to getting help, it's an incentive."

Even if a cocaine-addicted mother does not physically abuse her child, she may still be guilty of neglect, which can be just as emotionally damaging to a toddler or adolescent. "If you really are involved with drugs, you have little capacity for good child-rearing practices or nutrition. Drugs become your focus, your goal, and all other things secondary or tertiary to that," Johnson says.

"In some cases it's more neglect than abuse," Blume insists. "Mothers who are involved with alcohol and drugs alter their judgment; they'll make dinner when they feel like it and get around to the baby later. Time becomes unimportant, subjective."

Counters Weissman, "There is the stereotypical drug-abusing mother who neglects her child. But often there's tremendous caring about children, and many people find that hard to believe. Many women *do* feel guilty about their drug use, and children are frequently mentioned as the impetus for someone going into treatment or getting clean. They say, 'I didn't want to lead this kind of life for my kids. I wanted to set a better example.' But it's sort of a double bind because the daily responsibility to the kids then becomes the reason they can't go into treatment."

GETTING TREATMENT

Once a woman admits she has a problem and is forced to find help, no matter what the barriers, she must choose the best source of treatment. A 12-Step program, such as Cocaine Anonymous, is one of the best recommendations, particularly for women who do not have adequate financial resources, time, or child-care options to enter an inpatient program for a lengthy stay.

"Most people can be treated successfully as outpatients, especially women," Washton claims. "It's the place best suited to deal with a woman without disrupting her environment and family, especially if the husband is employed. Good, intensive, structured outpatient programs, running four or five nights a week, are one possible way around the problem.

"And the rate of success among outpatient programs is much higher than inpatient programs because the hope that somebody goes to rehab and comes back fixed or cured is an unrealistic one. Relapse rates after somebody leaves that protected environment are extraordinary. If you teach somebody how to say no to drugs in the real world, they progress a lot more quickly."

For women, however, any program—in- or outpatient—does have limitations. Many experts feel that women need to be approached in a very different therapeutic setting. "The model upon which these programs are built is a male model," asserts Kinney. "There are not enough services for women in the U.S."

Washton agrees. "The average, typical addiction-treatment program in Anywhere, USA, is still likely to be oriented toward males," he says. "In most big cities there are programs that have a special track for women or make a special effort to reach out for women, but I would say it's the exception to the rule."

"I may be another male chauvinist psychiatrist," confesses Cambridge Hospital's Khantzian, "but I feel I'm reasonably sensitive to the times we live in, and I know that women tend to feel more disempowered and disenfranchised. But once when I told a woman she was not surrendering to her healing process, she correctly admonished me that women have been advised all of their lives to stay humble and surrender, and it's gotten them nothing but more victimization and subjugation.

"We've got to find a different language for women, and maybe the anonymous groups sometimes miss the mark, preaching surrender and turning it over to a higher power. We may have to make allowances for these kinds of themes that have in some way ruined women's ability to manage their lives."

Says Weissman, "Most therapeutic communities have a confrontational approach to counseling—breaking down denial, defenses, etc.—and I think that approach doesn't work with a lot of women who are drug users. They have an extremely low level of self-esteem, and putting them into that kind of situation just makes it much worse. Unlike men, women aren't so much victims of their own denial. They just don't tend to identify drug abuse as the primary problem; their lives are a mess, and they're using drugs to cope. So breaking down denial doesn't really address the core issues, which are—and I hear this over and over again from women—a lack of self-esteem and no sense of power."

There have been some rehabilitation support groups established for women only, but primarily for alcoholism, which has had a much longer history and hence a longer time frame to develop new ideas. For example, the fundamental value of Women for Sobriety, a national program based in Quakertown, Pennsylvania, is an empowering one, "taking charge of our bodies, ourselves," as opposed to A.A.'s submissive philosophy of "turning over our will and our lives to a higher power."

Many experts in the field of addiction who treat women hope the emergence of such groups, along with the female tracks beginning to emerge in major suburban hospitals, are a symbol of changing times and attitudes.

WHEN WILL IT STOP?

Despite increasing efforts by the media, governmental agencies, and schools to educate the masses about the dangers of drug use, there has not yet been an apparent decline in the numbers of people becoming addicted. "The total population of addicts hasn't declined at all," says Atkinson. "I once heard someone in the alcohol-treatment field say that his job was pulling people out of a river where they were drowning. 'Unfortunately,' he said, 'someone else was throwing them in as fast as he could pull them out.' I think that's true of cocaine as well."

Most experts believe that just as we conquer one epidemic, there will be another to replace it. "Let's not kid ourselves," worries Byanka. "Something else will happen—because this is a drug culture. We've been taught not to suffer, and we use substances to make ourselves feel good."

Many hope, however, that a changing approach to education and the sophistication of today's teenager will someday make a difference. "I think the image of cocaine has changed," says Washton. "It's gone from being the chic, upper-class high, the Rolls-Royce of drugs, to being universally accepted as a dangerous addictive drug. I think people who use it are now aware that they're playing with fire. They may choose to do so anyway, but I don't think there is anyone out there who is still under the misconception that cocaine is a harmless drug."

Says Brotman's Meyers, "The answer to the problem is society and parenting, doing away with the hypocrisy of, 'Do as I tell you, not as I do.' Adults use alcohol, Valium, or cigarettes for nerves or Tylenol or codeine for a headache. Kids get the message that you need help to deal with life on life's terms.

"Kids are sophisticated today," he continues, "and we have to talk to them about what really happens, not use scare tactics like the 1938 film *Reefer Madness* or the recent TV commercial with an egg frying in a pan, with the voice-over line, 'This is your brain on drugs.' Kids know what's going on. They know people who have used coke for a long time and didn't die. But they have also seen people who have paid a heavy price and suffered serious debilitation."

Although women may have been the last faction of society to become enmeshed in the drug culture, they may also be the first to leave it behind. Theorizes Byanka, "I think women have a better social consciousness about themselves. They listen to drug education in a different way than men do and concern themselves with what's happening to our young people. Overall, I think women are still mom and apple pie; they worry about the future of their children, and that's going to factor heavily into abating the use of cocaine throughout our country."

ANITA

MOTHER AND CAR SALESWOMAN
MIAMI, FLORIDA

Anita, now 38 and living in Miami, has been sober since October 1983. She was married and extremely successful in car sales when, at 5 foot 3 and 89 pounds, her 16-year drug habit finally brought her down. Anita's addiction reached its height during her second pregnancy. When her daughter was almost 3 and her son was an infant, she abandoned her children to pursue using. Today she and her husband, Jim, are thankful that their children were born with no health problems and that they suffered no lasting consequences from Anita's erratic behavior. Anita is also thankful that Jim chose to stand by her. Without question, he saved her life. They tell their stories from both sides of the issue: those who are addicted and the people who love them.

Anita grew up in an affluent family that wintered in Pennsylvania and summered at a beach home in New Jersey. Her father, who had been an alcoholic for 20 years, owned a chemical company. Her mother raised six children, five of whom became addict/alcoholics. Although Anita's mother did not drink or use drugs, she was addicted to sugar, a problem that eventually caused her diabetes and ultimately led to her death.

Anita doesn't recall her father's alcoholism as being disruptive to the family, but he drank heavily, and she firmly believes in a heredi-

27

tary predisposition to addiction. Both her parents' families also had histories of drug and alcohol abuse. In her own case, her fear of obesity led to bulimia and initiated her drug use.

"I was obsessed with the fear of getting fat, and I ate more just because it was another compulsion/obsession," she recounts. "The first time I threw up was when I was 15. We had a housekeeper who was 16. We had eaten five tuna sandwiches apiece. We were stuffed, and the only way we could eat any more immediately was to throw up. So she drank vinegar, and I drank dish detergent. She threw up, and I didn't."

Anita never received counseling for her bulimia, although she practiced it sporadically for several years. It was the late sixties, and a high school girlfriend introduced her to a doctor who wrote illegal prescriptions for diet pills and diuretics.

As she says, "That was the first big problem. I was a senior in high school, sitting in history class, discussing it [bingeing and purging] with another girl in my class. She told me about a doctor who gave her and her mother diet pills. So although I was too young to buy alcohol, I went toddling off, and that's how I started using drugs. I went from 115 down to 104 in one week. The diet pills worked like a charm, but I became dependent on them to stay up all night to do papers that were due. I've never had a weight problem since, but I was left with the addiction to drugs."

Anita also began smoking marijuana the summer of her high school graduation and, influenced by the sixties, experimented with hallucinogens. Her experiences with LSD left her mentally incapacitated for an entire year and frightened her badly, but it did not deter her from continued drug use.

"During the summer, at a Doors concert, I took LSD. I did that probably a total of 20 times, which really messed me up. I couldn't remember from the beginning of a sentence to the end of it what I was talking about, and that was long after I had taken my last trip. Luckily, the material they covered during freshman year seemed to be a repeat of the material I had in high school."

A member of the high school honor society, Anita saw herself as basically a very straight, responsible person. Once she arrived at the University of Miami, her growing compulsion to drink and use drugs bothered her greatly. But she felt she was fighting a losing battle and figured she might as well enjoy it. She did—for a time.

"I always wanted to get sober," she emphasizes, the torment still apparent five years into her sobriety. "I went through a horrible time trying to control it in the early stages, but it became pretty obvious that I couldn't. The minute I said, 'I'm not going to smoke today,' I'd have an overwhelming compulsion to light up a joint. So I gave up and decided that I was going to enjoy it. I couldn't do anything about it; so why torture myself that way? But I was always worried about what I was doing to my brain, my body, and my life. And I remember thinking, 'Someday, probably in my early 30s, I'll figure out a way to handle this, to get out of it.' "

The changes in her life confused her greatly, but eventually, years later in a drug and alcohol rehabilitation program, it finally made sense to her. "I was absolutely outraged at what was happening to me," she remembers. "I didn't understand it. But later, when my counselors told me it was a disease, it made perfect sense to me. I know a lot of people don't believe that. They think it's just another excuse. But I tried to control it. I tried. The first time I ever drank, I was 16; I was in Paris, and I got drunk immediately. I never did any social drinking."

Anita's drug of choice was always alcohol, no matter how advanced her drug use became. Alcohol, she found, was a great enhancer for any type of high. But her next boyfriend, a serviceman whom she eventually married, introduced her to heroin and Seconal.

"I met a merchant seaman through one of my sorority sisters. He shipped out and returned in January of my sophomore year. He had just come from Thailand, and he had a whole bunch of heroin. It was absolutely a drug-dependent relationship."

Since Anita's dependencies did not truly worsen until she was away from home, her parents were not really exposed to her addiction. However, there was one incident that led to her arrest. Her new boyfriend, to pay off a $100 debt, gave her a pound of marijuana. She got busted for it. Her parents arranged, under the table, to have the charges dropped, but they still did not question her behavior.

"My father put together $6,000 in 10s and 20s and gave $2,000 to an attorney. All I know is that it didn't go beyond a hearing. The judge put the court on hold and he, the attorney, and the arresting officer, who was wearing all brand-new clothing, went into private chambers. I waited outside with my mother. The attorney came out and said, 'Okay, let's go,' and that was the end of that."

Anita's parents did, however, tell her they would no longer pay for her education if she married this man, so the twosome eloped. Their marriage remained a secret for some time, but eventually, after suffering her second bout with hepatitis, to which she was exposed by a heroin needle, the marriage came to light. She was forced to leave school and went home to live with her parents while her husband went to sea. Anita had never been hooked on heroin, but her addictions to alcohol and marijuana worsened.

Anita's résumé lists 30 jobs for this phase of her life, including manager of a paraphernalia shop, waitress, hotel manager, newspaper reporter, credit manager for a men's clothing manufacturer, gas station attendant, special-assignment policewoman, personnel executive, and pharmacist's assistant. She also sporadically attended Trenton State College, near her parents' home.

"I figured out I've had 30 jobs in my life, and I've been fired from half of them," she admits. "I quit the other half, or they just came to a natural end. Due to my drug use I couldn't hold on to some of the jobs."

In her early 20s, while working as a pharmacist's assistant, she stole small amounts of drugs and, when she felt she could fall under suspicion, began buying unclaimed prescriptions for her own use. It was also one of her earliest experiences with cocaine.

"Some of the older doctors would write prescriptions for eye medicine, so there was a jar containing an ounce of pharmaceutical cocaine with a federal narcotics $80 tax stamp across it. Sometimes the boss would have that out and ask me to hold down the store. He'd leave, and I always kept around straws, ostensibly for sodas. But of course it was really for the coke jar. I'd do a few snorts."

When her husband came to port, she would take a train to New York City to visit him. She relives one particularly harrowing incident: "I was in Harlem at six o'clock in the evening to buy heroin. It's the only time I've ever been in Harlem. I had my diamond wedding ring from Tiffany's in my mouth. There was a street fight going on, and some guy had his eye cut out. The police were turning the corner to go down there, and they just stopped dead and shone their lights on us. I guess it was pretty obvious what we were up to."

Anita later discovered that her husband was homosexual, and she divorced him. She had managed to progress to the last semester of her senior year of college at Trenton and was entering finals week with four As and one B, when she took off with a boyfriend for Acapulco, Mexico.

"We had full intentions of smuggling 150 kilos of pot back into the United States. I had somebody who was going to sell it in New England. I was going to use the money to finish my college education and to put myself through law school."

The deal went bad, and they decided to go to Las Vegas to try their luck at gambling. Looking back, it was lucky they did leave Mexico without the dope. Fifty miles over the border into Texas they were stopped, and the car was searched with dogs trained to sniff out drugs.

Once in Vegas, they lost everything, including the car, and spent the next seven months hitching freight trains home. It was one of her only periods of sobriety during her 16 years of addiction. The episode was also Anita's first and only endeavor to sell drugs. But overall, she claims, it was a good experience.

"I had always read about hobos on freight trains, and I thought that was really neat. Of course, I was 25 years old living out an 8-year-old's fantasy. But it was most invigorating. When we got back, I felt the best I'd felt in years, more alive, more healthy. Of course, I didn't have any money for drugs or alcohol. But I never dealt. I couldn't bring myself to part with any of the precious stuff."

Anita's addiction, at this point, was primarily marijuana and alcohol. She did pills whenever they were obtainable. "I would mostly go bar-hopping. I did a lot of that with my brothers."

Eventually, unable to meet eligible men and bored with her life, she decided to return to Miami, a much faster-paced city. It was the mid-seventies, and she quickly landed a job as a car salesperson, at which she was extremely successful and earned a great deal of money. It was on that job that she was formally introduced to cocaine.

"My father always wanted me to be an attorney. I thought I was too mollycoddled. I didn't think I was streetwise. And, of course, I thought being a car salesman was out of the question. But I sat down with a bottle of Johnny Walker and two of my college friends who were alcoholics. By the end of the bottle, it sounded like a great idea.

"I would sometimes go out with a customer on a test drive, and they would give me cocaine. I'd come back completely coked out. The thing is, if you're the type, you kind of know another addict. It's an irresistible gravitational pull. But it wasn't entirely constant. It was only during the last six months of my drug use that I was so highly involved with cocaine. I was doing a lot of prescription pills."

One evening she was invited to a party at the condominium of the vice-president of Ecuador, where she met her husband, Jim, now 46, also a highly successful car salesman. Six months later they married. Though Jim had done some experimentation with drugs, he never used heavily. They were a mismatched couple.

"Let's put it this way," Anita explains the situation, "Jim's father and twin brothers are alcoholics. He also has a recovering younger brother who's in Alcoholics Anonymous. So he was real comfortable around me. There is no mistaking how we end up with our friends and spouses.

"Plus, these guys think it's all fun—until you've been married to them for a while. Then they want to get serious. They want you to turn off the faucet. But it's like saying, 'All right, it's time for you to turn off your leukemia.' "

Jim, though unaware of the extent of Anita's drug use, agrees that his own dysfunctional family prepared him to accept his new wife's behavior as normal. "When you're raised dysfunctionally," he has come to learn, "your idea of marriage is sometimes not the norm. In my father's case, he was an advisor to the White House and one of the architects of the Geneva Peace Conference. He never drank anything but beer and never before seven o'clock at night. But it would change his moods, and occasionally it became really difficult. Yet he was a very good man, ask anybody. Just ask the family."

Additionally, Anita hid a great deal of her illegal drug use from Jim. A car accident some years earlier and a ruptured disk that frequently caused her incapacitating pain provided an excuse for her consistent use of prescription narcotics. And in the seventies few people questioned the use of prescription drugs.

"I would sometimes go on Demerol vacations," Anita jokes. "I'd go into traction in the hospital for a week. If I exercise, I can keep the pain under control, but I would use that to get drugs, and then the insurance, of course, would pay for the procurement."

"I had no idea that the amount of prescription drugs she was taking wasn't normal," Jim admits. "I thought if it was a prescription, it was okay. That, coupled with alcohol and then the use of cocaine, I was at a loss to understand what was going on."

As Anita's addictions worsened, her behavior became more and more erratic. She was able, however, to continue hiding much of it from Jim.

"I would get up in the night and go out riding around visiting friends, getting stoned, and sneak home at 4 A.M. I drove in and out of the driveway with my lights off. I'd glide in with the engine off. I'd climb back into my nightgown in the linen closet so my husband wouldn't know. One time Jim kind of rustled in his sleep, and I jumped back into bed with my clothes and shoes on and waited for his breathing to get steady again.

"But I was not a sex maniac. I was not out jumping into bed with guys who would turn me on. I was out pursuing my addiction. I was not a violent drunk, and I did not get into trouble. I always took cabs when I got drunk. I'd leave my $43,000 car wherever it was and get up extra early to go get it.

"I'd come in at 4 or 5 A.M., and it's hard to sleep when you're full of cocaine. Plus, you get this cocaine-induced psychosis. You hear a little noise outside and peek out the window. But I was holding down a full-time job selling automobiles, and I'd get up and be at work at 9 o'clock. I was functional. A lot of us are."

While cocaine was not her drug of choice, it was the most gripping drug and the one that finally brought her down. "Cocaine makes you think that it's your favorite drug," she explains. "Cocaine grabs you. You get high and then within 20 minutes you feel a drop, both physically and mentally. The high goes down in sudden drops, like an elevator; so you want to use again and again. But it really wasn't the best high for me."

What she did prefer was Demerol and something called a Brompton Cocktail, a mixture of codeine, morphine, and alcohol, often given to terminal cancer patients.

"The man across the street from our home was dying of cancer; so I would trade him pot for his Demerol pills because he didn't like them. And Brompton's elixir, that was great."

Four years into their marriage Anita and Jim had a daughter. Less than two years later, a son. During both pregnancies, particularly her second, Anita used cocaine and other drugs. To this day Jim has been at least partially unaware of that fact. Anita feels that he was in denial as much as she was. They are both thankful for the health of their children.

"If I had known she was doing coke, I would have been surprised," says her husband quietly. "If you ever saw Anita, she still looks like a college coed—a clean-cut, little blonde with a big smile. Very gregarious. She's not what you'd expect a drug addict to look like."

Anita counters, "I didn't exactly sit there and use it in front of him either. I had a walk-in closet on the side of the house where the maid was, and that's where I kept my coke. I'd go into the closet and shut the door, reach into one of my pockets hanging there, and snort."

Anita was in denial, but deep down she knew her drug use was entirely reckless, and she wrestled with the knowledge. "I didn't go out and buy a *Physician's Desk Reference* book," she relates, "because they were $25. Coupled with the fact I didn't want to have it lying around, because it was like real evidence. But I would run down to the bookstore and look up the various drugs I had gotten my hands on. If the book said, 'Yes, we know definitely that this drug does cause birth defects,' I wouldn't use it. I had that much control," she laughs. "But in most cases, they say it's not known if it will cause birth defects, and I would go ahead and use the drug, hoping that if they didn't know, it wouldn't hurt.

"I knew instinctively from the first time I went off to that diet-pill doctor that there had to be something wrong with all of this. It couldn't possibly be good. During my pregnancies I didn't drink and smoke. But I did cocaine, and I smoked hash and marijuana. I was stoned every day.

"I had 100 Demerol pills that I kept locked in my safety deposit box to try and keep them away from me. But every morning at 9 A.M., when the bank opened, I would be there to make my withdrawal. I was very fearful."

Although her children were apparently born healthy and normal, her drug addiction continued to worsen and, she admits today, her children were continually endangered by her addiction. "When my little girl and my little boy were teething, I would rub cocaine on their gums. I remember very vividly that my little girl was yowling all day long one time; so I took a little lump of cocaine and rubbed it on her gums in that spot. Almost immediately, I realized her yowling had turned into a song. She was really happy. I also remember with my little boy, I was just going to rub a little chunk on his gums, and somehow it zinged down into his mouth. It was more than I had intended to give him, and that upset me.

"Also, my little girl, at the age of two, would pester me and pester me because she wanted to have some wine too. I finally got a little, tiny wine glass. It was about the size of a shot on a long stem, and it was cut glass. So I'd put a little bit in there, and she'd like it and pester me for more. I know that she felt it, because then she'd go out in the living room and turn in circles.

"I felt bad that I was so paralyzed as a mother. My little girl would ask me a question three or four times, and finally she'd have to scream at me to get an answer. She started taking care of me at the age of two. I would forget my sunglasses and my purse. She would then scan the area and carry my things to me.

"I absolutely knew I shouldn't, but I was out of control. And that's the first step—your life is unmanageable. I was used to doing things that I didn't think were right. I knew that it was dangerous, and I was going to suffer from it. I really felt guilty, and I was so lucky because my son and daughter are perfectly fine. I discussed it with my counselor, and she said, 'You were at the height of your addiction then. What do you expect?' "

Anita recalls another occasion when her husband, a born-again Christian, was at church. Her housekeeper had the day off and she was alone in her bedroom, stoned.

"I was definitely incompetent. I remember smoking a joint and lying on the bed, all weak. I suddenly realized there wasn't a noise in the house. My kids were two and three, but I kept lying there convincing myself that of course the kids were still in the house. My brother drove up about 15 minutes later with them in his car. They had gone out of the house, around the corner, and they were with a man who was suffering from Alzheimer's. My brother just happened to come along. He was laughing and asked, 'Did you lose something?' They were better off with the housekeeper, who spoke no English. Spanish was probably my children's first language."

Whether or not Jim realized either the extent of Anita's addiction or the immediate danger to his children, he did finally confront her. "My husband told me to quit snorting or move out, and I very happily moved out," she remembers. "I decided it was too much trouble to raise the kids, run the house, and take care of him when it was much easier to snort cocaine to oblivion.

"I had a full-time, live-in maid, and my kids didn't need me as much as I needed the drugs, I guess. The drugs had priority. Also, my children didn't seem like people. They seemed more like objects because I wasn't human myself. I was detached. But there was this tremendous amount of guilt."

Jim, although he gave the ultimatum, was both stunned and devastated when Anita moved out. He was also left with two small children to raise by himself.

"I told Anita, 'You either go for help or leave.' She said, 'Well, I'll have to think about that.' I went to work. She called me and said, 'I've thought about it, and I've already moved.' I remember thinking to myself, 'What have I done?' I broke down and cried over it.

"I remember one day I was in the bathroom getting ready for work and just started crying. My daughter, who was not quite three yet, came in and said, 'It's okay, Daddy. I love you, and I won't leave you.' And she patted me on the back.

"I had guilt so strong—because we misplace guilt. We don't understand that we didn't do anything, addiction did it. I needed help too. But at that point, I didn't have Al-Anon."

While statistics show that men are much less likely to stand by an addicted woman than the other way around, Jim steadfastly supported Anita. "I really felt that Anita was on a banana peel. I would call her every day and say, 'The kids are fine. We love you. We want you to know that we're there for you.' "

Anita continued to visit her children but was highly irresponsible. Jim recalls one Easter she was scheduled to visit. She was expected on Saturday evening but didn't show up until Sunday afternoon.

"She arrived with big teddy bears and baskets for the kids like nothing had ever happened. By this time we had already celebrated Easter; so I suggested we go to the beach. She had left some clothes at the house, and she went and put on a bathing suit. I thought she had just gotten out of Auschwitz, she was that skinny. She looked terrible.

"When we got home, I went to help the kids get dressed, and when I came back, Anita wasn't there. I guessed she was putting her clothes on; so I went to see if she wanted to have dinner with us. I found her snorting in the closet, and I got sick to my stomach. I thought everything was going to be okay now, but nothing had changed. Just my perceptions."

By this time the 5-foot-3 Anita weighed 89 pounds. She had been living with her brother but later moved in with a co-worker who became her boyfriend and who supplied her with ample amounts of top-quality cocaine. Her thinking processes were, as they had been once before, dysfunctional.

"I wasn't able to eat. I leaned up against a BMW on the show-room floor one day, and I looked at myself and thought, 'I'm so skinny, if I catch a cold, I'm going to die.' I was coasting at work. I knew the job, and I was on automatic pilot. But I got to a point where I couldn't remember what I had said from one moment to the next. A customer would call me and say, 'I'll pick up the car to-night.' I'd say, 'Fine, I'll get it ready,' hang up, forget which car I was getting, and have to call back. Cocaine is the most devastating. For some reason it mixes you up so badly." Anita had also entered a new phase of her alcoholism.

"I'm so glad I got out when I did, because I've heard in A.A. meet-ings this gets worse. I would go to sleep and wake up in the middle of the night and have to have a glass of wine. I would wake up with the shakes. I was just beginning a very lengthy stage. People say it gets to where you wake up every half hour or less to get another drink until you're just drinking all the time."

Following Anita's Easter visit, Jim decided to make an appointment with the head of Addictionology Services at South Miami Hospital. Anita refused to go with him, but Jim said he was going alone any-way. Several days later, after numerous phone calls, she relented.

"I needed professional help to know what to do," Jim relates. "She said I was a fool. I said, 'Possibly, but that doesn't change the fact that I'm going.' But I went to work and got a call, and she said, 'I'm here at the house waiting for you.' "

"One day my husband called at work to say he had an appoint-ment with a doctor, and would I like to go with him. I finally went because I was so skinny," Anita says bluntly about her initial reason for seeking help. "I could see that I was just going to keep on snorting and losing weight until I died. I thought I'd go in, fatten up for 28 days, and get all strong and full of vitamins so I could go back out and continue. I had no intention of sobering up. I also couldn't allow myself to think. I couldn't cope with hoping it would work."

Recounts Jim, "We went, and that's when I really knew how badly she was doing drugs. The doctor started going through the different drugs that she did, and then Anita started adding some. I was just dumbfounded.

"Then the doctor said, 'Anita, are you an alcoholic and a drug addict? Do you want help?' Anita said, 'I guess so.' And the doctor said, 'That's not good enough.' Well, you could have knocked me over with a feather. I thought, 'What more do you want her to say?' But the doctor was looking for her to say, 'I need help,' not 'I guess so.'

"There was a silence for what seemed like an eternity. Then Anita said, 'No. I need help.' The doctor said she thought she had a space next week, then looked at me. I must have looked horrified. I was sure Anita wouldn't live another week in the condition she was in."

The following day the doctor found room for Anita, and they were able to admit her sooner than expected. Jim got a call at home, and it was up to him to go find her and actually deliver her to the rehabilitation program.

"It was my duty to find Anita somewhere; so I had to go to the boyfriend's house and knock on the door. That was probably the hardest thing I ever had to do in my life, facing this guy. Anita and I weren't together, and I did not believe the marriage was salvageable. I did this to save the mother of my children.

"I heard from Anita later. I had thought she would come spend the night or something, but she said, 'If I'm going into the hospital tomorrow, I'm going to go get drunk and high tonight. I'll be at the house in the morning.'"

Anita was admitted, but the counselors soon discovered she was a difficult case, reluctant to submit to the emotionally difficult process of recovery. They recommended her as a candidate for intensive, long-term treatment at Alina Lodge in New Jersey, where she spent 4½ months. Jim was forced to sell off real-estate holdings to help subsidize her recovery.

"My first week or two at Miami Hospital, I seemed to be thinking so slowly," she says. "My brain cells were depleted. They did an IQ test, and I came out 100 in verbal and 101 in math. I had taken an IQ test when I was 12 and had scored 138; so I was pretty horrified. You lose 7,000 brain cells every time you drink a martini, and they can find alcohol in your spinal fluid a year after your last drink.

"But I was so truly out of it that when I got to the hospital and they told us the rules, I truly believed in my heart that they were just suggestions. They told us we couldn't use any telephones for the first week; so the first day I sneaked over to the other side of the hospital and was just yammering away on the pay phone.

"It surprised me when the doctors and nurses said, 'You can leave anytime you want. Nobody's keeping you here.' It surprised me because I had never said anything about leaving. I never had any intentions of leaving. During the first week they were suggesting long-term treatment that wasn't so stringent. But by the end of the second week, they were saying it's either Alina Lodge or nothing.

"I couldn't believe that 28 days were going to offset 16 years of drinking and using, but I went. Alina Lodge was extra strict for reluctant-to-recover types. They knew where you were every second. As soon as you get there, they assign you a buddy, someone who's been there a couple of months. They have rules, and they give a person with this disease exactly what we need, a lot of structure and no nonsense.

"We weren't allowed to get away with anything. Women weren't allowed to talk to the men at all. You were up in the mountains where there's nothing anywhere around, but you weren't allowed off the pavement. I used to write letters home saying it was incarceration."

The program that helped Anita also reached out to Jim. That's where Al-Anon came in. The program recommended that all family members go.

Says Jim, "I remember walking in, and I didn't know what caused the tightness of my chest, difficulty sleeping, tightness in my stomach, irritability, sore back, sore feet. I had to get rid of the blame, get rid of the pity, and move on. I had to begin my own recovery. I had to begin getting well—understanding that this was a disease, and I was not involved. It was important for me to be in a group that understood."

Today Anita remains in a once-a-week "After Care" program. She also regularly attends meetings of Alcoholics Anonymous. Jim continues to attend Al-Anon meetings. Anita is also back in college but unsure of what profession she wants to pursue. She is in a liberal-arts program, considering law school.

"You know, what your addiction doesn't take away from you, your sobriety will. I thoroughly loved selling cars while I was stoned, but it was apparently something I needed to be drunk and stoned to enjoy. Sober, I hated it. So I went back to school. And at the rate I'm going, my college career will have spanned 21 years, which I've heard is typical for an alcoholic/drug addict. We have a very hard time finishing things. Somebody will decide to paint the room, and do it all except for maybe one wall.

"I originally went back for premed. But my husband had a little bit of surgery on his back, and I discovered that I'm not suited to be around drugs. He was walking around with some poppy products, some sort of codeine. I was okay for about three days. But he was leaving them out in sight, and he'd rattle one out in the morning and one in the evening, and all of a sudden, I wanted to take one. I told my husband, 'Please don't let me know you have those pills.' It really scared me.

"But I think about using every day. This is not willpower. It's your spiritual condition. Also a good memory of how bad it really is. But it took me about four months or so to lose that horrible compulsion to use, and for the first year or so I could have easily gone back."

Anita also realizes how lucky she was to have a husband who stood by her throughout her addiction and who helped her achieve sobriety. As she explains, "Women will stay with a drunken man, but the men, when their wives get too drunk all the time, will just dump them and go find somebody else. I have a very unusual husband."

Experts claim that it takes as long as seven years for an addict's thinking processes to return to normal. But Anita and her husband see a definite, steady improvement.

"She's more sure of herself. She's in college, she's trying to improve herself, and she tries to be a good mother," Jim says. "To her credit, she's giving it her best effort. I'm very fortunate. My business is terrific, I have two great kids, Anita is trying hard in recovery, and I've got a beautiful home.

"Not everything is good, no," he admits. "There are a lot of things I could really say are the pits. But I've got to understand that I cannot mold Anita into what I would like her to be. I have to accept her as she is and grow to love it. I had conditional love. I had to learn *un*conditional love."

He downplays his own credit and attributes much of his caring to his deep religious faith. "If you would have told me years ago, 'Jim, this is what you're going to go through,' I'd have said, 'Pass.' But I got married for better or worse, and I made that promise a long time ago. Maybe you need to check my sanity level, but I believe that the price is worth it. The kids have a mother who's alive and well.

"So if the marriage ends tomorrow, and it could, it was worth it. You're going to laugh at this, but God chooses your partner to help you get to heaven, and I'll be honest with you, Anita has certainly helped me to get to heaven."

"It will take a long time to get my thinking normalized," Anita predicts, "but I've come a long way. It's slow, but I see a huge difference. I've been told by other people in A.A. and the After Care counselors that there's a difference. I seem to be able to cope a lot better, to handle things, not to let things slide.

"I keep thinking I could be having a lot more fun," she laments, "but then I ask, What do I consider fun? And when I think about it, fun is being drunk. So I haven't really redefined my ideas.

"But," she adds, "I have taken up golf."

YVONNE

PHYSICIAN
NEW ENGLAND AREA

Yvonne, now 34, grew up in a severely dysfunctional alcoholic family and left home at age 16 when she became pregnant. Determined to show her abusive father that she was somebody, she received a degree magna cum laude in biomedical engineering. She then went on to medical school. She was introduced to cocaine socially but soon began using it to deal with the stresses of marriage, raising a small child and the long hours and hard work that were the medical-school routine. At her worst she was using more than a gram a day and, despite her background, took the drug sporadically during her second pregnancy. She considered suicide but didn't want to leave her children alone. Finally, no matter what the consequences might be to her career, Yvonne knew she had to get help. Today she is an emergency-room physician and medical director of a large addiction-treatment program in the New England area. She also lectures other physicians on recognizing and treating the emotional, spiritual, and physical symptoms of addiction in their patients and themselves.

"I had never done anything in my life. I occasionally had some alcohol, but I drank socially and never did anything inappropriate. I think part of that was a reaction to my father's drinking when I was a child. I never wanted to use any substance, because I saw it destroy our family."

Yvonne's mother was a housewife until she was forced to begin waitressing to help support the family when Yvonne was in the fifth grade. Her father, who had once owned a successful printing company, lost everything because of his drinking. After that he occasionally sold vacuum cleaners, encyclopedias, or cars.

Yvonne was the middle child of three sisters, but the oldest sibling was blind and was often away from home at special schools. Their mother worked nights, and Yvonne and her younger sister were alone at home with their father. "There was a lot of physical violence, but it was also not an emotionally safe place to be," Yvonne remembers. "My mom would go off to work, and I was in charge of making dinner. My father would drink and then get angry over nothing, like the way you washed the dishes or the way you cut your meat—absolutely ridiculous things. You couldn't do anything right.

"He often hit me inappropriately, and he would scream and give us big lectures. He told us we were worthless and that his life would be perfect if we had not been born. Great things for self-esteem. Many times I would run away at night to my best girlfriend's house and call my mother at work. She would pick me up at 11 o'clock or midnight.

"But nothing was ever said—it was just denied that this was insane behavior. I was always mad at my father, but there was a part of me that knew he was sick. I always hoped that he would get well. But while he was crazy, the person I had the most resentment toward was my mother. She was too afraid to leave."

In her midteens Yvonne became pregnant and ran away from home to marry the father of her child. She was determined to be a better parent and to prove that she was a capable, worthwhile human being, despite what her father had told her.

"There are different roles that a child takes on in a dysfunctional household. There's the scapegoat, who feels like everything is her fault and acts up frequently in school. There's the clown, who tries to lighten things up by always being silly, never taking anything seriously. And there's the overachiever, the caretaker. I fell into that role. I felt that I was responsible and that if I worked hard enough, I could make things better at home. Of course that never happened.

"I basically ran away from home at the tender age of 16 and have been on my own ever since then. I was pregnant, ended up marrying the father, and had a daughter. Then, when she was two, I went to engineering school. I worked very hard trying to be the perfect mother and the perfect engineering student. I did very well. I got my B.S. magna cum laude in biomedical engineering in 1977 from a prominent school in the Northeast, when Emily was five."

Yvonne worked for a year in engineering but applied to several medical schools and was accepted at a prestigious school in New England. It was during her first year there that she and her husband first experimented with cocaine.

"Matt and I were introduced to cocaine socially. Friends brought it to the apartment a couple of times. The first time I tried it, I remember being very fearful. My first question was, 'How do you know I'm not going to be allergic and die?' The other thing I asked was, 'How can you guarantee I'm not going to become addicted?' I was a total nerd.

"This was the late seventies, and people were saying it wasn't addictive. I remember the first night we shared a gram with another couple and had a few glasses of wine. We chatted all night, and I thought it was the cat's meow because it made me a Chatty Cathy. I had always been very hardworking and very determined but also very shy. I started talking.

"Right after the first time I used it, I asked that we put aside part of our monthly budget for a gram of cocaine a month. Matt didn't like cocaine, but he didn't mind if I did it, because it was so sporadic. Over the course of a year I may have bought it six or eight times. And everything else was going fine in our lives."

But after her first year of medical school Yvonne began to feel weighted down by so many responsibilities taken on at such a young age. She decided to divorce the ever-reliable Matt.

"My husband was a very gentle and kind man but somewhat passionless about life and about us. I got married young and had really missed my teenage years. I was always either at home with my daughter or at school. I felt like I had not experienced a heck of a lot of life. There was a whole big world out there, and the type of love I had from Matt wasn't enough. It was a very working relationship, but it wasn't very exciting. I wanted my freedom to experience life. We separated on friendly terms."

During her second year in medical school, at age 24, Yvonne became more social and began dating a man who was considered on campus to be a real catch. Both the parties and the relationship helped escalate her cocaine use.

"I started doing things I had never done before. When I had a night free here or there, when Emily was spending time with her dad, I started to go to parties. I ended up dating this gentleman who turned out to be a big drug dealer at school. But I didn't know that when I started seeing him. He was a very popular, athletic, Waspy man who came from a family of doctors, and to be with him was supposedly something special.

"Coke was an accepted part of a lifestyle for him and his friends. Certainly it was a part of our relationship right from the beginning. For me it was great. We went dancing or stayed up late and chatted. It was a very social drug."

But that period didn't last. Cocaine soon became more than just a social aid; it became a way to get through the day, and it disrupted her life. "That year I used it not only on weekends, but also at night to stay up and study," she says. "Now it wasn't just a social drug, I was using it to get work done. That's when I began having problems. I became sleep-deprived and nutritionally depleted."

Looking back today, however, Yvonne feels that she was most likely addicted from her very first inhalation. "When I tried the drug for the first time, it really did something for me," she reflects. "It made me feel the way I had always wanted to feel my whole life—free, happy, and as good as everybody else. Even though I had been achieving and my life was perfect from the outside, my inner feelings were those of someone suffering from the disease of chemical dependency.

"I always felt less than I was, out of place, and fearful. I thought that it was a big trick or joke that I had gotten into medical school and that I was dumber than everyone else. I felt that at any moment everything was going to come crashing down. When I did cocaine, it was an escape from that reality. It made me feel good."

By the end of her third year of medical school the pressures had mounted enough to make Yvonne consider suicide. The action, she explains, was more of a cry for help than a serious attempt on her own life.

"I was actually thinking of dropping out. I couldn't admit I had a problem, because my close friends were not drug users. I could use an entire gram in a night, but I hid my drug use from them. I only used with this guy I was dating and his bizarre friends.

"I didn't want to do coke, but it had gotten to the point where I knew I couldn't *not* do it. It was affecting my life, and I didn't know where to turn. My option was a suicide gesture. I took just enough aspirin to make me sick but not enough to kill me. I wanted to kill myself, but I couldn't because of my daughter."

The "suicide gesture," however, did get her help. She met with the medical school's chief of psychiatry and admitted to him she had a problem. "I told him I had a problem with cocaine and that was why I tried to kill myself, because I was very depressed. With cocaine, after it makes you high, you keep doing it, and all it does is make you very wide awake and depressed.

"He said he didn't think I was suicidal, but certainly I couldn't do the drug anymore. He told me I had to change my life so that coke wasn't a part of it anymore. I agreed, took a month off from school, stopped seeing my boyfriend, stopped using the drug, and started to get my life back into order.

"But looking back, the big surprise is that the doctor never told me I needed to go to A.A. I saw him in therapy for a while, and I told him about my family. He just told me to distance myself from my family and not to do alcohol or drugs. Well, I may have been off substances, but I was still stuck with the same feelings of low self-esteem. It's inherent if you have the disease of chemical dependency."

She entered her fourth year of medical school and, almost immediately, fell in love with another intern. They were married eight months later. But he was addicted to marijuana and later became abusive.

"Part of being a woman, especially if you don't feel good about yourself, is accepting unacceptable behavior. That was as much a part of my disease as using substances was. Our marriage, which lasted four years, was basically a marriage in which he was high every single day. Plus, he was an abusive person, just like my father.

"About a year into our marriage I picked up cocaine again. I had started my internship, and I was trying to run a house, take care of Emily and work 80 hours a week. I used cocaine as a reward and started doing it on weekends again so I could do the housework.

"It was also an act of defiance. I had told Paul before we got married that I had a problem but that I was clean and not doing anything. He said, 'No problem, just don't ever do it again.' But when our marriage started to deteriorate because he was just never emotionally available I thought I would hurt him horribly by doing this.

"Of course, I ended up hurting myself. I did it very sneakily. I felt guilty. I knew it wasn't good. Yet once I started again, I was back into the whole routine."

Yvonne's drug use continued for the next two years. She had graduated from the four-year medical-school program and was in her second year of a three-year residency. Her use of cocaine was not quite as heavy as before, but it was just as steady. And then she became pregnant.

"Even though I may have been doing just a gram a week, I was emotionally involved with the drug, waiting to buy it and keeping a very tight budget to do it," she remembers. "I was doing it intermittently, but I was still using it in an addictive way, which was that I did it on the sly as an escape. I wasn't doing it socially, I felt too ashamed. I knew it wasn't good for me.

"In the marriage I was in, we were addicted to each other, and we were each addicted to our own substances. Then I became pregnant. Being pregnant is bad enough, but along with working in a hospital 80 hours, trying to run a house, it was horrible. And occasionally I would do cocaine."

It was the early eighties, and not much was known about the side effects of cocaine use on a fetus. Although something in Yvonne's training told her it couldn't be good for the baby, she used cocaine on and off during her pregnancy.

"There weren't many statistics out on whether or not it would do fetal damage, but in my mind, I knew that it caused vasoconstriction—which is clamping down of the arteries—and that could somehow affect the placenta or the baby. But I wasn't doing a tremendous amount."

The baby, named Jennifer, was born in ostensibly good health, and Yvonne decided to take a year off to be with her newborn. She occasionally worked a shift in the emergency room to supplement their income.

"I think what kept my drug problem under control for so long was the fact that I had so many responsibilities. I always had to get to work, drive Emily to school, etc. But I was trying to control it from the beginning. I felt the lack of control and the need to control all at the same time. And I felt guilty. It was horrible, just hell."

Yet Yvonne, as a physician, was afraid to come out in the open and ask for help. There was, she explains, too much at stake. "The thought that a physician would do drugs was incredible. There was a lot of self-reproach involved with that. On the outside I supposedly had everything—a career, a husband, children—but I was still miserable on the inside."

Yvonne did manage to control her drug use while breast-feeding but weaned the baby as soon as possible so she could resume using. By now she was back up to half a gram a day. She says, "Here was a year that I was home, and the only person I really had to answer to was an infant. It gave me the space and time for my addiction to run wild."

Yvonne's husband more or less knew something was amiss but never connected the problems to cocaine use. "He suspected something was wrong with me. I had such mood swings and stayed up so late. But you also have to realize that he was in residency and smoking a lot of pot. It was the most dysfunctional family unit I've ever seen in my life. There was no emotional or spiritual connection between us. There was anger, and there was occasional play. I can't believe we both lived in the same house like that."

Yvonne was a highly functional addict, both at home and on the job. She never actually used cocaine while working but feels it still affected her performance in more subtle ways.

"I never actively did drugs while I was on the job. I was a nighttime, isolated abuser. But I would say my emotional stability was affected by my having done drugs. When it came to interpersonal relationships, especially with other interns and physicians, I was always coming from a defensive, angry, guilty place rather than just being in the moment and learning the most that I could.

"I think people knew something was wrong, but they didn't know what it could possibly be because there wasn't as much drug awareness then. But when you're nutritionally depleted and sleep-deprived, your general health goes down; your energy level, what your skin and hair look like. I did not look well—I always looked like I had a viral infection or something. I had sinusitis a few times, and I was emotionally on the edge.

"But I had a lot of excuses to be stressed out. I was a resident, I had a child already, I was pregnant, I was married to a man everyone knew was a drug addict. Everyone thought it was a miracle I showed up for work every day, but nobody suspected me. So if I ever cried at work or got angry, it was assumed that I was doing too much and that I just needed more time for sleep. There's also the denial that's prevalent in our society.

"Today I do a lot of consultancy work for corporations like Texas Instruments about impairment on the job. But for myself it's very difficult to say whether I suffered any cognitive or motor-skill impairments secondary to what I was doing at night—mostly because I was off during the year of my worst use. And when I was using at medical school, I didn't have primary responsibility for anyone; I was part of a group. I can look back and say I don't think I made any serious errors as a result of my drug use.

"I also made sure that things were always done for the children during the day. I am a very compulsive person. The house was clean, there was food, we each got to work. I used only after dinner. Then I would allow myself.

"I always bought from the same person. We would go for a ride with the kids; I would pretend it was a social visit and pick up the cocaine. Then, once they were in bed, I would sit up, do cocaine and just drink."

Her drinking was increasing dramatically in direct proportion to her escalating cocaine use. Toward the end she was drinking about half a pint a day of amaretto, rum, or vodka.

"I started to drink more and more because the cocaine would make me so wide awake. The only way I could possibly fall asleep, the only way to rest before the next day, was to drink. It took away the jitters. So I would drink and do cocaine. It sounds so sick," she laughs today. To further complicate matters, Yvonne developed kidney stones, an extremely painful affliction, and her newborn was diagnosed as having a heart defect that would require corrective surgery.

"I started passing kidney stones and was supposed to have surgery. But in the meantime I was placed on Percodan by a urologist. So at this point in time I was either doing cocaine or taking the Percodan that had been prescribed.

"Jennifer also needed heart surgery. Her ligamentum arteriosus had not closed at birth, which is a complication of a cesarean. But before they knew what had caused it, I went through a whole bunch of guilt, thinking that it was my cocaine use during pregnancy. That was a horrible nightmare to live with until the diagnosis."

In addition to the obvious stresses, one of the excuses Yvonne put forward to justify her drug use was the continuing deterioration of an already abusive marriage. So when Paul left for a Tennessee hospital to study pediatric trauma for a month, Yvonne decided that it was her opportunity to sober up.

"I thought the reason I was using again was my husband. I knew I had to stop; so I figured, 'Here's a month he'll be gone and I'll be able to quit.' I did stop using cocaine for the entire month, but it was a constant battle; nothing on the inside was healed."

Shortly after Paul returned, his behavior worsened considerably, and Yvonne was more miserable than ever.

"Paul was only violent when I would demand things from him that he didn't want to give, like time with the children or helping around the house—or because of my mood swings from cocaine. Over the last year there had been a couple of incidents with him slapping and pushing me. Right after the baby was born, he would get stoned and disappear into the sunset. When he came home, I would yell at him, and he would turn around and meet my anger with violence.

"I can't believe I lived that way. But I felt I was just lucky to have someone in my life. The thing is that I was very smart, I was kinda fun, I was pretty. But the inside of me felt like what my parents had always told me when I was little, which was that I was inherently no good. My self-esteem was so screwed up that I accepted unacceptable behavior just to be with somebody. It's like *Women Who Love Too Much*—total insanity."

One day when Yvonne was working a shift at the E.R., she was the victim of an incident that made headlines across the nation and that forced her to re-evaluate her life.

"It was a turning point when I was the victim of a violent crime in the emergency room. A guy came in with a machine gun and held a bunch of us hostage for two hours. The SWAT team was there but never quite made it in. The siege ended when a nurse and I jumped this guy. We handled it very well, and it was in all the newspapers. But what happened that night while the guy was pointing the machine gun at me was that I realized I was more afraid of my husband than I was of the man with the gun.

"The next day, Paul beat me up again. I turned to a female friend who was a pediatrician and told her what the hell was going on in my life. We went and got a court order to kick him out of the house."

But getting Paul out of her life took care of only the most superficial of Yvonne's problems.

"He basically disappeared from my life and from the lives of the children. I was left with a sick baby and a sick me. I started to do cocaine like you wouldn't believe. The last three weeks I was using, I would say I did a gram, gram and a half, a day.

"After Jennifer and I both had our surgeries, my cocaine use zoomed completely out of control. It got to the point where I would be up late at night wanting to die and knowing that I couldn't commit suicide because I had children. If I did it, they would be at much higher risk for suicide themselves. But I would write notes and think about it. That's how calculated it was. And I was afraid to tell anybody. I thought I was bad, not sick. I thought I should have complete control over this, and when I didn't, it meant I was a defective person.

"Because of TV advertising, I started calling Alcoholics Anonymous and the 1-800-COCAINE hotline. I told them about my problem, and they started convincing me that I was sick and needed treatment.

"A lot of what kept me out of treatment was that I was too embarrassed. I thought that as soon as I went for help, I would be ending my career, and I had worked very, very, very hard. Nobody ever told me that A.A. was an anonymous program. I thought the minute I walked into an A.A. program that I was busted, that everybody in the city was going to know, and that I would no longer be a doctor. And a lot of who I was was what I did.

"I finally decided, in talking to people on the hotline, first things first. I needed to get myself well before I could be a mother and before I could be a doctor."

As important as her career was to her, Yvonne based her decision more on her desire to be a good mother. "If I dropped out of medicine, it would be no great loss to anybody," she philosophizes. "But being a mother, it's almost as if you're blessed if you have healthy, wonderful children. And their lives are really your responsibility until they leave you. They were mine. I love my kids, but I was not able to take care of them, and it was driving me crazy.

"When I left home as a teenager, I tried to raise Emily with a lot of the things I felt I had never gotten as a child, a lot of support. I was always a good mother, but now I was frequently short-tempered, and I hated myself. Oh, God, I hated myself—because it was the one thing I had always said as a child I would never do. And yet here I was.

"Being a physician, you can isolate emotionally. You know how it is—you always hurt the ones you're closest to. And in medical school we had no indication about drug addiction spiritually. We learned about what happened to the liver, what happened to the heart, but we never learned about the disease concept. We never learned that it was a three-fold disease of feelings and spirituality as well as physicality.

"Until I got into treatment, I really thought I was a very bad person. But it got to where I knew I was going to die, and, therefore, being a physician didn't matter."

Yvonne had made the first step toward getting help but still had several major hurdles to overcome. Her ex-husband was far from supportive, and she was supposed to resume her residency in a few weeks.

"About a week before I went into treatment, I called my husband and said he needed to come take the baby. I told him I had to go away because I was a drug addict and I needed help. He said, 'If you do that, then I'm going to go for custody of the baby and ruin your life.' But that just didn't matter anymore. I knew I wasn't going to have a life if I didn't get help.

"I called the resident chief of medicine and said, 'I'm not going to be there.' I had left in excellent standing when Jennifer was born. Because I always felt so bad about myself, I had always worked compulsively hard. So I was an overachiever on the outside, and people never suspected. They just thought I was a hardworking, occasionally moody woman who seemed to be handling way too much. The chief of medicine said, 'Go, stay as long as you need to stay, and then come back.' "

But while she had now gone too far to turn back, Yvonne was still reluctant to commit herself to a detoxification program.

"At that point, I think I needed to be removed from my environment, from trying to sober up with the kids around and without any help," she recollects. "My family wasn't there, because what usually happens in an alcoholic home is that people scatter, and that's where my family was. The only connection we had was on the phone, and it was always everyone trying to blame everyone else for how horrible we all felt. It was more destructive than helpful because nobody had started to heal yet.

"I couldn't find anyone who would take me to treatment, because nobody believed I had a problem. So I drove myself. The treatment center was three hours away, and I did that round trip three times in one day because I couldn't commit myself. I would drive up to the gate and say, 'I'm not an alcoholic or drug addict who needs to be put away.' I just didn't know what was on the other side of those doors. I had never seen one of these places.

"On one of the trips home I had thrown my suitcase down the cellar stairs and said, 'I'm not going.' I had scheduled admission for one morning and finally showed up at three o'clock the next morning.

"I had been drinking and doing cocaine during the whole trip. God saved me on the road. When I walked in the door, I was a mess. I didn't have any money or clothes with me. Over the past couple of months I hadn't been eating a lot, and I was very skinny. I was also agitated from the drugs.

"At the point I walked in the door, I was what every typical drug addict or alcoholic is like. I felt that if the world had been nicer to me, I wouldn't have the problem. I also felt like a very bad person. But they just met me with open arms. I celebrated my 30th birthday in treatment, and it was the nicest thing that ever happened to me."

Yvonne didn't have the physical side effects of withdrawal that many cocaine addicts have in response to a dual-abuse problem of narcotics or a far more extensive drinking problem. She did, however, suffer the emotional withdrawals.

"Cocaine doesn't have a physical withdrawal, but it has a psychological withdrawal—with drug cravings, drug dreams, and a lot of paranoia and guilt. Certainly I suffered from all of those symptoms. And the depression that sets in once you come down from cocaine.

"Cocaine causes massive releases of dopamine in the brain, a chemical that causes the euphoria. So the first week off the drug you're dopamine-depleted, and it's a real crash. Therefore, even if the most wonderful thing in the world were to happen to you, you wouldn't feel real joy because your brain's depleted of the chemical it needs to feel that emotion. You sleep and eat a lot.

"I also wanted the drug more than anything and knew that I could never do it again. I felt like I would never feel good unless I did it. But day by day the dopamine levels increased, and I did feel better.

"It was a major point of reflection in my life. I was given back myself; I was given a feeling of hope for the future. Certainly I was not responsible for being a drug addict, but I was accountable for the things I had done. My responsibility was recovery, and that wasn't really going to begin until I left treatment.

"What that meant was starting to live an honest and clean life and going to A.A. meetings. I still go to four or five meetings a week, and I need them. Recovery is a continual process. I also saw a shrink for a couple of years to work out a lot of my adult-child issues."

Even while undergong the initial process of becoming sober, Yvonne's thoughts turned to ensuring that she could continue to practice as a physician.

"While I was in treatment, I called the state medical society, anonymously at first, just to test the waters. I finally admitted who I was, where I was, and what my problem was. For a couple of years I went to the methadone clinic to give a urine tox screen in front of a witness. It was humbling to say the least, but it was worth it to me. With cocaine, because it's such a powerful drug, you need a little more help to ensure your recovery."

After four weeks at the inpatient recovery program Yvonne returned to complete her residency. Her sobriety greatly enhanced the rest of her training.

"It was a much nicer experience because I had the program to help me deal with the people I worked with. What A.A. gives you is not just sobriety, but a way of dealing with life on life's terms; so you don't buy into the insanity, and you don't start feeling like a piece of crap when someone else feels they need to make you feel bad.

"I did it just the way A.A. says to do it, one day at a time. I didn't project into the future about how tired I was going to be or what people were going to say. I did what I thought was right in every situation and lived with it. It was a whole different ball game, and it was wonderful. I think everybody who's going to be a resident should go to A.A. and learn how to live. There are the 12 Steps of recovery, but they're almost like Buddhist principles. It's really neat."

Although she approached it with an optimistic outlook, Yvonne did feel that there was more of a stigma attached to being a female addict than a male addict.

"Men are supposed to go out and build monuments and bring home dinner. Women are supposed to be home sitting on the eggs. Women are supposed to be able to nurture and take care of the people around them. And I don't think that's bad—*somebody* in society has to take on that role—but it doesn't leave a hell of a lot of room to get sick. Even when my ankle was in a cast once for six weeks, I still had to do laundry, cook food, go to work, etc. Whereas if I were a man in a relationship, I think I would have been pampered.

"I think a lot of people associate being in an altered state with being sexually loose. I never went out and drank in bars or picked up men or even got sexually excited about cocaine. But I still worry today about what people think of me, even when I speak at A.A. meetings sometimes. People assume that because you had a problem with drugs, all your morals have suffered."

Despite that fear, Yvonne has been very up front about her former drug problem with co-workers and patients alike. "Every place I've worked since residency, I've always told them that I'm a recovering alcoholic/drug addict. That's my bottom line."

Though her professional performance was never questioned and she sought help on her own, Yvonne herself suggested that she undergo a five-year program of random drug testing. "I carry a beeper when I'm on the job," she explains. "They beep me, and I have 24 hours to go to the chief of medicine's office and give urine with his nurse as a witness. I told them that I need to do this for me.

"I had never gotten into any legal difficulties, but if I had, the state medical society would have demanded that I do urine tests for five years. Because of malpractice and litigation potential, I think I will probably do it forever. I think when people act irresponsibly, they should be taken out of their position. But on the other hand, I see why physicians get sued, and there are people who are just trying to make a buck. The state medical society would back me up if necessary.

"Most people are very wonderful when you tell them you are doing something to stay well and grow. They don't attach a stigma to it. But there are other people who are uneducated and uninformed and who assume that you're a bad person."

Though the stigma of being a physician who was addicted to drugs initially kept Yvonne out of treatment, today—as someone who lectures other physicians on addiction—she feels that the rate of doctors and nurses who are chemically addicted is higher than anyone wants to acknowledge.

"I went to the American Medical Society's conference on impaired health professionals about a year and a half ago. The statistics are that as many as 50 percent of physicians and nurses are adult children of alcoholics who suffer from the syndrome of low self-esteem. In order to compensate, a lot of them took on the role of caretaker. While the general population has an incidence of alcoholism or drug dependency of 10 to 12 percent, among physicians and nurses, it's 15 to 20 percent."

Some experts estimate that addiction among health-care officials may even go as high as 30 percent, attributable to both the stressful nature of the job and the sheer availability of drugs.

"First of all," explains Yvonne, "physicians are under a lot of stress. They never learn to take care of themselves, particularly spiritually and emotionally. They also have the added burden of working in a system that says you are what you do. It's not your essence, it's not that you're just an inherently good person because you were put on the planet.

"In medical-school residency you don't get rewarded for what you do right, you just get punished for what you do wrong. You get fed up with the hours, lack of sleep and money, and the bad personalities of the people you work with. A lot of these people are emotionally sick." She also points out that physicians are incredibly reluctant to diagnose their patients' addiction problems.

"Physicians don't like to diagnose their patients as alcoholics or drug addicts because most of them consider it a moral issue. They will assume anything, even in the face of elevated liver enzymes or motor-vehicle accidents under the influence. They'll even write out 'scripts' for tranquilizers to deal with the agitation and depression.

"I now lecture area hospitals about the disease concept. If you change your attitude about what it means, then you can approach people with love, and it's a treatable disease. It doesn't mean that you'll ever recover completely, but there's remission if you go to A.A. and don't use.

"You have to take what I consider the Middle Eastern approach to medicine, which is about spirituality and healing: healing the person rather than just the body. Even the American Medical Association defines alcoholism and chemical dependency as a threefold disease—emotional, physical, and spiritual.

"But a lot of male physicians don't want to hear about that. They want you to identify the biochemical marker that diagnoses it. I think women take the person more as a whole; their environment and their life. We've been socialized to do that."

Yvonne is in debt today for $60,000, mostly attributable to her schooling, but she estimates that $15,000 went for cocaine.

"I started off badly because I put myself through school. I've never had any financial help from anybody. But during the last six months I was using, I took out a home-equity loan to support my habit. During my first year in recovery I paid that off because it made me feel so horrible to owe money for something I had already done that was so bad."

As Yvonne points out herself, recovery is a continual process, but her life today is already dramatically improved. A.A., she continues to stress, has helped her learn to live life on its own terms.

"Life has inherent risks," she concludes, "but some people are not willing to assume them. They want to blame everybody on the planet for everything that goes wrong in their life. I mean, when you're born, you're going to die.

"I'm not saying I'm not an alcoholic or a chemically dependent person. I think there are physiological differences among people who become addicted, and someday we will define them. But I think the main reason I began using was that I didn't know what was normal in life, what I should accept, and what I shouldn't.

"I thought I wasn't worth anything, and the anxiety that brought had to be medicated. I hadn't healed or recovered from my childhood, yet I was trying to be all these things in a society that is so demanding. Something had to go.

"I can look back on my life this way now. Certainly, while I was in the middle of it, before I was educated, I had no idea what was wrong with me. I just knew I was different. Part of it was trying to prove my worth, that I had a right to exist, that I wasn't bad, that I was good. And I was going to prove that by taking care of the whole world."

Yvonne may not be taking care of the entire world today, but she's certainly doing her share. Right after this conversation, in fact, she was on her way to Honduras to provide medical assistance to children less fortunate than her own daughters.

"We're setting up a freestanding clinic for 10 days. A bunch of physicians, dentists, and ophthalmologists are going down with medicine and equipment. Most of them are recovering addicts. Part of recovery is developing that spiritual side of you. And it just feels good."

MONICA

HIGH SCHOOL TEACHER
MIAMI, FLORIDA

Monica, currently 33 and the mother of two small children, now trains schoolchildren to be peer counselors. She was in her early teens when she started to use coke, at least partially to control her weight. By college graduation, when she began teaching high school history, she was a heavy abuser, addicted to alcohol, Quaaludes, and cocaine. She was also bulimic. Although she was almost completely ineffective as a teacher and used steadily on the job, she was never confronted by either the administration or her peers. In fact, no one even seemed to notice. In the end she weighed 89 pounds, was in failing health, and was completely out of control. At age 28 it was a failing marriage and a near-death experience that finally brought her to her senses after 12 years of using. Today, sober since 1984, she draws on her own experiences to help sober up kids before they go as far as she did.

"The other night I worked the A.A. hotline," she sighs. "People call in desperation. I was talking to a mother whose son is heavily into drugs. I said, 'The best thing you can do for him is not let him think that he's snowing you, like everyone let me think.' I wish in retrospect that my parents or my husband would have confronted me, given me an ultimatum. Everybody knew, but nobody ever said anything."

Monica recalls that from an early age she was unencumbered in her use of alcohol and drugs. When she was 16, her father was an engineer for a petroleum company, and she was living in South America, where cocaine is as readily available as Coca-Cola.

"I first started smoking pot. But shortly after that some guy turned me on to cocaine, and I fell in love. I wish it would have been horrible, but I loved it. It did for me what I couldn't do for myself. I was always a little heavy, and it enabled me to control my weight. It also gave me a lot of self-confidence that I didn't have before."

At the time Monica didn't think she was doing anything truly wrong. It was not, she contends, a staged rebellion against overly restrictive parents.

"It wasn't that big of a deal. It was illegal, but almost all of the kids did it. It was very cheap. I never really looked at it as a rebellion. Maybe in a way it was an 'I'll show you' kind of thing, but it wasn't a conscious decision. It was more that it did something for me that I couldn't do for myself. It made me feel better about me. But then it got to be physically addictive."

Her parents were not users, and they frequently questioned her behavior throughout high school and college. But they never actually tried to stop her. Monica earned straight As in school, and so, afraid of what they might discover, her parents simply ignored the issue.

"My father drank, but it was normal drinking. My mother is very vehemently against drinking. She drinks wimpy drinks, like pink ladies, I think she calls them. Those fruity kinds of drinks. But she'll have one, and that's it.

"There were incidents in South America when they couldn't wake me up. And I would come home drunk. But they didn't want to know. Then I went away to college, and they didn't have to see it. Plus, they always lived overseas, not only in South America, but in the Middle East and Europe. I was in the States, and we were very far apart. So it was real easy to hide from them. I would go and see them on vacation, but it's very easy to maintain for two weeks.

"But they knew. One time when they were visiting me in Florida, I had no intention of doing drugs. Then a friend of mine gave me Quaaludes, and I ended up taking them. I was out of it. There was a lot of crying and 'Please stop doing this.' I felt bad and was real remorseful, but it didn't last. I said, 'I'm so sorry, and I'll never do it again,' but as soon as they left, forget it."

Monica was once stopped by a Florida police officer for speeding while obviously stoned, but he didn't intercede either, she laments. "My ashtray was filled with roaches, and I was so high on Quaaludes that I couldn't even drive. But the cop didn't arrest me, because I reminded him of his daughter. At the time I thought that was wonderful. It's easy to say this in retrospect, but maybe putting me in jail, having to go through that, would have helped me sooner. I don't know."

Though Monica had begun her college education at Tulane, a prestigious school in Alabama, she quickly transferred to the University of Florida, where she knew it would be far easier to obtain drugs. With little effort she was a top student, but she admits her education was hardly a priority at the time.

"I picked that university because I heard it was the number-one party school in the country, not for any educational benefits. Cocaine was very easy to get. But I don't think addiction had really taken a strong hold of my life at that point. I got straight As, and I pretty much had it together. We primarily did coke on weekends. Cocaine is the type of drug on which you can still function if you're not using excessively. My heavy usage came later on."

Even so, a good friend from Monica's brief days at Tulane recalls that her drug-taking was still pretty heavy. She visited Monica in Florida and was repelled by the change she saw in her.

"It was a much wilder school," relates Lisa, who experimented with drugs and alcohol but was not a regular user. "I never knew if it was just a weekend of partying or more than that. Every time I went to see her, she was more involved. We grew apart. I mean, we were friends, but not the same type of friends. She changed a lot. We were just living different lifestyles."

Monica began to seek out friends who also partied heavily and it was in this setting that she met her future husband, Barry, who consumed a great deal of coke. They both agree that the relationship was initially based on mutual attraction—not to each other.

"We probably wouldn't even be together but for our mutual use of drugs," Barry, now 37 and an attorney in Miami, says matter-of-factly.

"It was definitely a drug-dependent relationship, although it grew into something else," Monica admits. "The people that he ran around with were people with whom I wanted to hang around. It was his lifestyle that I liked. He had a lot of friends who were big-time users, and I knew it. He was also an attorney and a real nice person, but the draw was definitely more than that."

"I never knew where Barry stood," interjects Lisa. "As a friend I always wondered if he was a stimulus to what she was doing, due to his lifestyle. It was never that I didn't like Barry, but you get mad."

Directly out of college Monica landed a job as a high school history teacher in a Miami suburb. She wasn't a bad teacher from the start, she maintains. It was a very slow descent into insanity.

"Coke made me feel like superwoman, like I was better at everything. I could do anything and say anything, and I'm sure I thought that translated into the classroom. I probably convinced myself I was a better teacher.

"I taught for about three years under control and for about three years out of control. It was the last three years of my using when it really got out of hand. But it was a gradual progression. There wasn't just one day when I woke up and said, 'I know today that I'm a shitty teacher.'

"But I always knew in my heart. I used to think, 'God, Monica, you really have a drug problem.' Then I'd go, 'Nah,' and I'd pour myself another drink or do another line. I just didn't want to face up to it. I almost thought it would go away. I don't know what I thought, but I never thought it would get to the point that it did."

When she was 27 and at the height of her addiction, Monica married Barry. According to Lisa, the couple was high on a lot more than love. The occasion was a fiasco.

"Monica called to ask me to be her maid of honor, and of course I said yes. They married on New Year's Eve in New York City. We were all pretty buzzed, but she was as high as a kite. She was doing tons of coke and drinking tons of champagne. She and Barry were so high, the justice of the peace didn't even want to marry them.

"They had a big dinner reception at the Palm afterwards, but Monica spent half the evening in the bathroom. That's also when I realized that Monica was not only a major addict, but bulimic as well. Barry kept yelling at her, not so much for the drugs, but because he would make her eat, and she would go to the bathroom and throw it up.

"After their marriage I was so upset with the Monica I saw that I could barely talk to her. It wasn't the Monica I had known, and I was just devastated by the whole thing. It was just a horrible, horrible evening. We talked every couple of months after that, and I used to tell her I was concerned. She told me not to worry, that everything was okay."

Monica was drinking heavily, beginning in the morning, and doing coke in the school bathroom, as much as several grams a day. She also used narcotics to take the edge off. She recalls chewing Big Red cinnamon chewing gum to hide the alcohol on her breath.

"I didn't necessarily do coke in the classroom. I went to the bathroom, probably five or 10 times a day. I had an aide, and she covered. I'd put an assignment up on the blackboard and leave.

"I was definitely drunk at school, but I never drank at school. I drank in the morning before I went to work. I drank at lunchtime. I drank immediately after work. But I never had a bottle, per se, in my desk.

"I would go to bars after work and drink martinis. A fifth would probably be a fair estimate. My drink of choice was a Stoli martini— straight vodka with a couple olives on the side to kill the taste. I called it a martini, but it was shots of vodka. It's the way we play with our minds: because I was drinking a *classy* martini, it was okay.

"I was eating Quaaludes too—to take the edge off the coke. That's also why I drank. You get too hyper, and you don't want to be shaky, you just want to be high. We had Quaalude doctors here. You just told them that you couldn't sleep, and they would give you a 'scrip' for 100 Quaaludes. I went to five doctors; so I was taking about 500 a month. I never got them from the street."

It was Miami in the seventies. Cocaine was less expensive there than in other cities, but even so, Monica and Barry admit that it added up. "It was a lot of money, believe me. But his money was our money, and then my money was my money," she says, explaining that her entire salary went for drugs.

Monica claims that no one ever suspected what she was up to, neither the school administration nor her aide, who worked with her very closely. With the exception of a few close friends, her husband verifies that this was probably true. But just perhaps, Monica allows, her students may have known all was not right.

"I was probably slurring like crazy, but nobody really questioned me. The administration deals with 100 teachers. They hire you, and as long as you do your job, as long as the kids are kept under control, they don't really give a shit.

"I think the kids suspected, but they never said anything. Maybe it was paranoia, but I always had that feeling. We weren't that far apart in age. I was teaching seniors, kids who were 18 years old. I wasn't that much older.

"There were a few friends who sometimes said jokingly, 'Remember the night when you did such and such?' I wouldn't remember it at all. I'd be momentarily embarrassed and remorseful. I'd say, 'I'll never get that high again.' But only until the next time."

Monica feels that the subject she taught, history, also enabled her to escape detection. Despite the fact that she was a popular teacher, she regrets that she slighted the education of so many students.

"I remember going to work, the kids coming in, and classes changing. I remember doing my lesson plans and all of that, but it just wasn't that important to me. They definitely didn't get the education they deserved. I didn't do the job. I really didn't teach. History is pretty basic, just dates, figures, and people. It's not like dealing with a psychology, philosophy, or English class. It's not like I had to grade creative writing or an essay.

"I gave them assignments and told them to do their work, and that was it. 'Read the chapter and answer the questions at the end,' I'd say, or 'Summarize the chapter.' I gave them work sheets, that type of thing. Then I had kids exchange papers and grade each other. Or I had my aide do a lot of it. I was too involved with my own thing. I'd just sit there and veg out.

"High school seniors like it better that way. I was very well liked. They probably thought that I was a great teacher because I didn't hassle them. Today I expect a lot more from my students."

Monica applied just as little effort to giving her pupils their year-end grades. It was, she admits, an almost random process.

"You just give grades," she shrugs. "Nobody really scrutinizes you, and you cover your own rear end. You give a couple of Ds, a majority of Cs, some Bs, and just a few As."

And her lifelong ability to organize helped her compensate for being stoned, both in the classroom and at home. "It's funny, I'm more forgetful today than I was when I was using. I think because I knew that I was so out of it, I created a network to remember things. I wrote everything down. I was much more conscious of my appointments and fulfilling obligations. Now I'm not so worried about it, because I don't have anything to hide. Just today I forgot a dentist's appointment. The girl called, and I was completely oblivious. I was shocked. In the old days I would not have done that. I covered up everything.

"Most of my friends just didn't know," she continues. "One of my friends says she was always amazed at how normal I appeared. It really blows her mind because I always had dinner parties and played the role of a lawyer's wife. My house was always neat. I'm a good cook. I always prided myself on taking care of my home and my family. Some addicts let their homes become pigstys, and they don't take care of themselves. That never really happened to me."

"Monica *was* out to lunch," Lisa confirms. "But she is also extremely bright and extremely responsible. She just always made it a fact to do what had to be done. She always found the strength or direction. It doesn't surprise me that people at school didn't know, and I'll bet that she was never a very bad teacher."

Despite her successful front, Monica did eventually begin to feel paralyzed as a teacher. The compulsion to use, however, overwhelmed her guilt. Finally, rather than stop using drugs, she stopped teaching.

"There are ways to justify anything. There are a lot of poor teachers, and I probably used to think I wasn't any different. An alcoholic or an addict doesn't care, but the thought used to cross my mind. It was my bottom per se. I felt that I was burnt out, and I decided that I didn't want to teach anymore.

"I started working for a computer company and I made a lot of money. I did a lot of traveling and a lot of entertaining, taking people out to lunch to sell systems. That's when my drinking really progressed. I would drink all day on the job and drink myself to sleep. It got really bad. I thought they were going to fire me; so I decided to quit. They were shocked because they thought I was doing a good job. But I thought I was doing a shitty job. I guess that had a lot to do with my own lack of self-esteem."

Now that she was home and not working, drinking and using became Monica's only occupation. And it was now full time, rather than part time.

"I was drinking and I was using constantly," she reveals. "I bought ounces of coke and just did them all day long. I was always using more than Barry. I would do just as much with him, but then I would go into the back room and do my own too. It was an excessive amount."

Monica and Barry had freebased off and on over the years. Most experts agree that cocaine, already highly addictive, is even more so when smoked. Snorting, however, remained Monica's favored method of ingestion.

"We had friends who lived in Colombia, and we would take bad coke and remake it into good coke," Barry chuckles. "It was like playing chemistry."

"But that wasn't what I loved the most," Monica pipes in. "I enjoyed doing that, but I much preferred snorting because the coke goes further. 'Basing is an instantaneous high; the rush is very intense. It is a better high, but it goes away very quickly. That's why it's so addictive, because you want to do more right away. Whereas when you snort coke, it lasts longer. You're not doing it every five minutes. You're doing it over a longer period of time.

"Also, 'basing really frightened me because it is very, very addictive, even more so than snorting. I could see that in other people who weren't normally addictive. I could see it in Barry. He and the people I was friends with were getting very obsessed with it. I think that deterred me as well."

Though Barry was using heavily, as much as 10 grams a day, he ventures to guess, he maintains to this day that he was not an addict. Shortly before Monica became sober, he was able to stop using cold turkey, with no help or counseling.

"We were smoking about a quarter ounce a night," he admits, "but it didn't interfere with whatever I was doing. I probably denied for a long time that I was addicted. Even today I don't think I am. The fact that I stopped using myself supports that view. But I remember sitting around a table for days on end. And if you look at it objectively, if you would have seen me at three o'clock in the morning with a pipe in my hand, knocking on people's doors, you would say that I am an addict.

"But I just stopped," he continues nonchalantly. "At some point I just didn't like it anymore. Seeing Monica get more addicted, visualizing her reactions, made me want to stop. She'd say, 'I didn't get my share. I want more.' She would steal it from me or anyone else."

Agrees Monica, "I think that probably had a lot to do with it—because he was so averse to me, and I was just so disgusting at the end. He quit a few months before I did."

Though there were confrontations, Barry never gave Monica any ultimatums. As he grew more frustrated, however, there were incidents of domestic violence. Monica, an obviously strong-willed woman today, says that at the time she felt she deserved the abuse.

"We used to fight about it. He used to say, 'You're a drug addict, you're doing too much.' I would try to watch myself and maintain for a while; then I'd go out of control, and we'd have another fight. That pattern went on and on, but he never really confronted me. He never really gave me an ultimatum. I think he was afraid of what would happen, that maybe I would get out."

"Those episodes *were* confrontations about using," Barry counters. "She was in denial, and she'd lie about doing it. She'd be eating Qs [Quaaludes]. I'd be at work, call her up, and she'd be slurring on the phone, saying, 'bl, bl, bl, bl, bl.' She'd make me run home from work and beat on her."

"I remember isolated incidents," Monica says. "I was never hospitalized, and it was never anything visible. I do remember me saying something, and him slapping me across the face.

"Today I will barely put up with him raising his voice to me. But at the time I hated myself so badly, I thought I deserved it. I remember rationalizing it and thinking 'Yeah, I am a piece of shit. Sure, go ahead.' I can definitely see how women can be battered and not object if they have such low self-esteem, which is what I've had all my life.

"When I look back, I think he did it out of frustration, and I really don't blame him at all. He was probably at wit's end and didn't know what else to do."

Barry, unable or unwilling to help Monica, drifted away. He is unable to explain, however, why he didn't leave. "I was just detached," he shrugs. "I was probably away a lot is the answer. I wasn't home. I really didn't have any place to go, but I was gone in my mind any-way." The way Monica looks at it, though, he was always there for her, no matter how bad it got. "He was very supportive, and he's wonderful. He truly is. I wouldn't have made it without him. To be perfectly honest, I wouldn't have put up with what he put up with."

Shortly before the end, self-controlled Monica was cracking up and Lisa recalls several pleas for help. From several thousand miles away, her friend tried to come to Monica's aid.

"Once, out of the clear blue, Monica called me and just broke down on the phone," Lisa relates. "She called me two or three times in a two-week period, just falling apart. She knew she was going down the drain. The cocaine hotline had literally been introduced that month. I dialed 1-800-COCAINE to find out how I could get help for Monica in Florida when I was in New York. It must have been right before the car incident. An addict has to hit bottom before she can get help, and Monica had."

It was "the car incident" that almost ended both her marriage and Monica's life, at age 28. It was, however, what got her, indirectly, into a treatment program.

"At the end I was just emaciated. I weighed 89 pounds. I wasn't eating. I was just doing coke all the time and drinking. My husband and I were in the process of moving, and I was going back and forth from the house that we were living in to this brand-new town house we had just bought. I was taking days just to put the paper in the cabinets.

"One day I looked in the mirror. I had been sweating, and my hair was all matted to my head. I remember saying, 'I don't even know you anymore. I don't know who you are, and I hate the person you've become.' I literally went into a closet and did every bit of coke that I had. I didn't even chop it or anything. I was just snorting rocks, and they were falling out of my nose.

"Barry came home from work that day and went to take a shower. I got in my car, and I have no idea to this day where I was going. I drove into a ditch across the street, and I tried for 45 minutes to get the car out. I kept putting it in reverse, and I just remember looking at the trees and everything else.

"What happened is that I overdosed and had a seizure. My hus-band finally heard the car and came outside. I had bitten the inside of my mouth and my tongue. Blood was streaming out, and I was screaming at the top of my lungs. He tried to get me out of the car, but I wouldn't. So he did the only thing that he knew to do and called the police."

Barry still recalls the incident with considerable disdain. Even his wife's near demise didn't break through the wall he had built around his emotions.

"She finally went crazy. She was in this ditch convulsing, and she wouldn't open the door. But I didn't call help first; I moved the contraband. I thought she was dying, and I'm sure I cared, but I wouldn't have lost too much sleep over it either. Sounds great, doesn't it? But I would have lived either way."

When the police finally arrived, Monica had come down from an out-of-control high and was somewhat calmed.

"By this time 45 minutes had passed. I had pretty much screamed and sweated most of the coke out of my system, and I got out of the car. The cops told my husband he had better get me to a hospital because I was in pretty bad shape. He took me, and they said I had suffered a cocaine overdose. They sent me home with a bottle of tranquilizers. I couldn't believe what I had done. I was mortified, embarrassed, and humiliated. Barry wouldn't talk to me. It was real, real bad."

But instead of going for help, Monica went on a two-day binge, during which she blacked out. It was, she admits today, basically a suicide attempt.

"For the next two days I drank constantly—champagne, as a matter of fact. I decided that if I was going to go out, I was going to go out with a bang, and I drank nothing but champagne.

"It's funny because when my Visa card bill came, there were liquor stores on there that I have no idea where they are. And I never found out. I just went out and bought. I just drank and drank and drank. I was in a blackout for two days.

"Finally, on the third day I made beef stew, although I don't remember doing it. When my husband came home, he found me on the kitchen floor passed out in the beef stew. Still in denial himself, he thought that I had suffered a concussion from the accident. So he called the rescue squad. They came and told him, 'The woman's drunk.' They took me to a hospital, and I slept through the night. The next morning I woke up, and a doctor we were friends with was

there. He said, 'Monica, the next time I see you, you're going to be on
a slab. You're killing yourself.' I looked at him, and for the first time I
said, 'I need help.'

"Later, Barry went through the garbage because I had hidden everything outside. He started pulling bottles out of the Hefty bags, and
there were 20 or 30 of them from those couple of days."

Monica was admitted to a drug-rehabilitation program directly
from the hospital and, upon her release, immediately began attending
both Alcoholics Anonymous and Narcotics Anonymous meetings.

"I didn't want to die, and I knew that if I ever used again, I would.
I had come so close, it was like a near-death experience. Lots of people experience a rebirth, and I believe that's what happened.

"After five weeks of rehab I started getting more self-esteem and
believing in myself. I realized that things had to come from within.
Outside forces weren't going to fix me or help me. I had to do it, and
that's what I did. I did everything I was supposed to do. I went to 90
meetings in 90 days. I got a sponsor and did all the things they suggested to me. It's been five years, and I haven't had a drink or a drug
since. I don't even take Tylenol. When my son was born, I didn't take
painkillers. I'm about as clean as you can possibly be."

Though she was never counseled for her bulimia, she no longer
practices today. Even so, Barry recalls that it continued for quite some
time into her sobriety.

Today, Barry feels the experience of Monica's drug abuse left a
mark on their marriage, but Monica says it pulled them closer together. "We've been together 12 years, and he's always been there for
me. He really cared. I think it brought us closer together. If he stuck
with me through that, we can probably go through anything together."

Now the mother of two boys, a newborn and a 4-year-old, the one
thing Monica continues to regret about her addiction is two abor-
tions. "I didn't want to stop using drugs, and I knew I would have to;
so I elected to terminate both pregnancies," she reveals. "I've had a
lot of guilt over that. I think, I could have a child such-and-such an
age. I probably made the right decision by not bringing a child into
that kind of atmosphere. But at the same time your heart asks, 'God,
why did I have to be so fucked up?' "

The positive side, however, is that she has channeled her experiences into being a good teacher, training kids to be peer counselors. She is often saddened by the state of today's teaching industry.

"I didn't do anything when I was using that's not being done in the classroom today," she laments. "There are coaches who teach, but sports are all they really care about. There are teachers who show movies and read the newspaper in class—and I don't think it's necessarily because they're addicts or alcoholics. I just think there are a lot of poor teachers out there.

"I'm a counselor today, and I work very, very hard in my job. I'm real dedicated, and that's the way I make my amends. There's no possible way I can find all those kids and apologize to them. The way I make up for it is to do the best job that I can today."

She feels that her own experiences, though she doesn't discuss them with students or co-workers, make her a top-notch counselor. "I do an excellent job, and I know it. I'm very good because I care, and many teachers don't. I teach children how to counsel other kids. We deal with drug and alcohol problems, abuse, that type of thing.

"I talk about my experiences, but I tell the stories as if they happened to another person. To do otherwise would be professional suicide, and I'm not willing to risk the years that I have in the school system."

She knows now that teaching straight is much easier than doing it while being stoned—a fact she wouldn't have believed at the time. "It's much easier. I'm going into class with a clear mind and a willingness that I never had before. I love what I do. That's the reason I started as a counselor. I know; I've seen it, and I've lived it. I don't even have to ask.

"I've started believing in myself. I have a new dedication to be the best that I can."

KELLY

**RETAIL MANAGEMENT EXECUTIVE
SEATTLE, WASHINGTON**

Kelly, now 34, came from an
alcohol-abusive family. The psychological distress, she realizes
today, was directly related to the development of her eating
disorders as well as those of a younger brother and an older sister.
Kelly was an anorexic/bulimic, earning her bachelor of science
degree when she tried her first drug, an over-the-counter diet aid
called Dexatrim. Not only did it help control her weight, but Kelly
liked the heart-pounding high. She later advanced to speed and
eventually cocaine. To take the nervous edge off her drug use, she
began drinking low-calorie white wine and later vodka, which she
substituted for food. Allergic to alcohol from day one, she was a
severe blackout drinker, rarely remembering where she had been or
what she had done—including three car accidents, one of which
almost killed her. She was, however, highly functional in general,
and few people suspected her addiction, including co-workers,
friends, family, and her live-in boyfriend of three years. Eventually,
at the height of her addiction, she was doing a gram and a half of
cocaine and drinking a half-gallon of vodka a day, and she was no
longer able to hide the truth. Her brother finally intervened and
had her hospitalized, five years after her initial introduction to
drugs. It was a difficult battle, but today her drug addiction, her
alcoholism, and her eating disorder are under control. She has been

sober since 1981, arrested her bulimic disorder in 1982, is happily
married since 1985, and counsels other people with eating disorders
in a southern California branch of the Rader Institute, the nation's
pre-eminent treatment group for such problems as anorexia,
bulimia, and compulsive overeating.

"My father's still in denial," sighs Kelly as she examines her past, "but there was a lot of alcohol abuse in our home when I was growing up. He drank a lot, and my mother enabled him to do so."

Her father managed the service department of a car dealership, and her mother was a housewife. Kelly and her younger brother and older sister, looking for a way to deal with the dysfunctional family life, all became compulsive overeaters.

"My father's alcoholism pretty much permeated my life and was the reason why I didn't want to drink," she recalls. "Instead we acted out our feelings with food; it was readily available and became a social event. All gratification for us came through food. We came from a very small town, our parents had married young, and it was real old-fashioned. Nobody ever talked about feelings. Kids were to be seen, not heard. We used food as our outlet.

"We all three have eating disorders, but none of us knew that then. Mine didn't start until college. I was an anorexic/bulimic. I was always skinny, whereas my sister was 200 pounds. She was a compulsive overeater pretty much all of her life and developed bulimia later. My brother was a bulimic who began in high school."

Kelly didn't start using drugs until the second year of a two-year college program when, for the first time in her life, she gained weight. "I was 20 years old and had never dieted before, but my metabolism changed. I started to gain weight; so I tried Dexatrim. Diet pills were my initial drug—I never drank or used drugs prior to that. But doing them led me to speed, which is just a more potent form of Dexatrim. I went on a crash diet. I lost an incredible amount of weight and became anorexic, not knowing what it was at the time."

Kelly was now hopelessly trapped in the conflicting worlds of self-starvation and bingeing. She either fasted completely or consumed as much as she possibly could. Eventually, to take in both worlds, she became bulimic and began abusing laxatives.

"I was compulsively eating and would then become anorectic through self-starvation. But now I wasn't able to strictly fast or compulsively eat. Those things went in cycles; so I began purging myself."

Soon after that Kelly graduated and landed a job as executive manager of a large, well-known department store in the area. She was 21 and making $30,000, an admirable salary today but even more so in 1977. It wasn't long before a male friend, a recreational cocaine user, introduced her to the drug in a social setting.

"Through experimentation I found I liked coke. It gave me more energy, and not only did I feel good, I lost my appetite. It worked for me. But it was never a status thing, and I never experienced that real euphoric feeling, just the knowledge that I could control my appetite and that it kept my weight down. I think that's more common than anyone realizes. There's definitely the high and the illusionary thinking. But I think a lot of people use coke strictly for weight control, and then it starts to cloud their thinking. They rationalize, 'It's not really that expensive or that harmful.' "

In the beginning her coke use was rather light. "Just whenever somebody had it around or when we wanted to splurge and treat ourselves," she says. "It was just enough to combat the weight, and I was very much in control at that point."

To take the edge off all the stimulants she was using, Kelly began drinking low-calorie white wine. Although she found she was allergic to alcohol, she continued to drink.

"During my first experience with drinking, it wasn't a controlled feeling, and I got drunk very quickly. I was allergic from the onset and went into an immediate blackout. But I found I could drink a little less and use more cocaine, which enabled me to drink more. Nobody knew the insanity that was going on in my life, and I had one more secret."

Eventually, low-calorie wine was no longer enough, and she began drinking hard liquor, despite its caloric content. She simply substituted booze for food.

"I was so strung out, I needed something to come down. When I drank, I said, 'God this is great! I'm a little chemical gourmet here.' But I needed more and didn't know why. So I began drinking tequila or vodka. I rationalized the calories because that was all I would have. Sometimes I mixed it with grapefruit juice—but I didn't eat lunch or dinner. That's the insanity of it. You're just not thinking clearly."

As her drinking progressed, so did her cocaine use. Within two years of her initial snort she was using heavily, but she says her memory of that time is too cloudy to recall the extent of her habit. "I did cocaine with my friends, but I did three times more than any of them even knew. It was purely a means for me to keep going, to survive my eating disorder. Right after I began drinking, my weight became uncontrollable, and I had to use more coke to combat that."

Although she was living with a man who was a mortgage investor, Kelly began dealing coke with some friends, behind her boyfriend's back. They deluded themselves into thinking that it was okay, she says, because they didn't sell to strangers.

"It wasn't really big time, just enough to cover our own usage. We just sold it to our friends, and nobody else knew. I was using cocaine with people in three-piece suits who no one would have ever guessed the truth about. We all lived in condominiums on the waterfront in Lake Washington, and that's where we dealt. But that was the delusion. It didn't matter what we told ourselves, we were actually dealing drugs. I didn't do it very long."

For more than two years Kelly was able to keep her addiction and alcoholism a secret, despite the wide-ranging swings of both her weight and her mood.

"I would go without sleep for three or four days. I was out there, but I didn't realize it. Cocaine gave me the feeling of being in control of my life when in actuality I was out of control.

"Nobody ever knew what kind of mood I'd be in from day to day. Plus, I'd fluctuate 10 or 20 pounds within a week's time. People would say, 'Oh, you're gaining or losing a little weight,' but nobody asked what was going on. People constantly told me how good I looked, even when I got too thin. No one ever confronted me."

Kelly had few side effects of her drug abuse but did once seek medical advice for shortness of breath. "I went to the doctor, but I didn't tell him what I was doing. So he prescribed me Valium for nerves. But I didn't like it. You weren't supposed to drink with it, and I was afraid of what would happen to me if I did. Plus, it calmed me down, and I liked uppers."

Although Kelly tried to keep her drug life separate from her career and her romance, her lifestyle slowly began to take its toll. She now used at least a gram and a half a day, and her drinking continued to escalate.

She was never arrested for driving under the influence, although she frequently drove during her blackouts and was once stopped by a state patrolman who locked up her car and took her home because "he was being nice—or so he thought." Kelly was involved in three car accidents, each of which totaled her vehicle, and none of which she can remember to this day.

"I only went out when I drank. I drank at home, but then I would get into blackouts and leave. I don't know where I went or who I was with, but I would always come back. One time I borrowed a friend's car without telling him, ran into somebody or something, and knocked one of the doors off. I returned it without a word. He had to tell me about it later, but he never got upset with me.

"The third time I was in a *terrible* car accident. I don't remember what happened, because I had been drinking and was in a blackout, but the story I gave the paramedics was that a car swerved in front of me and I swerved to miss it. It's really foggy to me, but they didn't even do a blood test, and I was never charged for anything.

"I was driving my boyfriend's BMW, which had an entirely steel frame. But it was totaled. I hit the windshield and split my head open. I had over 100 stitches from my eye to the middle of my head. I also gashed my knee open. It's a 100 percent total miracle that I'm alive."

Kelly also believes that the accident speeded her final descent into uncontrollable addiction, although it was another year before she bottomed out entirely and was pressured to seek treatment. "I truly believe that the car accident contributed to and facilitated my addiction. I was functioning and in some sort of control before that. But from then on everything went downhill very quickly. It gave me an excuse for what was going on in my life, even the blackouts. Plus, I really believe that when I hit the windshield, I lost some sense of reason."

A few months later, unable to hide or control her behavior, Kelly decided to break up with her boyfriend, with whom she had lived for several years, and buy her own condo.

"The guy I was living with had no idea what was really going on in my life, God love him. He didn't have a clue, so how sick do you think he was? But I was very functional until the end. I hid my ad-dicton from him, and I apparently acted fairly normal even when I was blacked out.

"But when I moved out after three years of living together, I gave him no reason why, and he was totally shocked. I just suddenly said that I had decided I couldn't live with him anymore. He was in a three-piece suit on his way to work and said, 'What?' I got my own place and never spoke to him again.

"I just wanted to get away from people. They were bothering me. I was having mood swings and was literally crazy, but I never associ-ated it with my drug use, and I never associated moving out with the fact that I wanted to use uninterrupted."

While Kelly wouldn't admit—or didn't recognize—that she had a drug or alcohol problem, she knew something was amiss. Less than a year after moving out on her own, she felt that she was "going crazy" and went to a neurologist to seek help.

"I didn't know why I kept doing what I was doing. I'd wake up every morning and say, 'Okay I've got to stop this,' but then I'd reach for my cocaine or take a drink. I knew something was wrong, but that's the insanity of the illness. You don't associate it with the drugs for more than one brief second. There may be a moment of clarity, but then you use the drug to stop thinking about it. It's so insidious.

"I thought I was crazy and needed a brain scan. But what I told the neurologist was that I was losing my memory, that my hair was dry, brittle and falling out, that I was tired, and whatever other excuses I came up with. I didn't tell him I was drinking or using drugs. I couldn't ask him if I was insane, and I never told him my real fears were that I couldn't stop eating and drinking.

"The doctor thought my problems were from hitting the wind-shield. It seems really strange today that he didn't pick up on the real problem. But to my memory, although I was in such a fog, he never asked any questions. He ran EKGs on me, which came out fine, but he gave me some pills for possible epilepsy. I didn't take them."

What the doctor did recommend was for her to take a leave of absence from her job. Her boss didn't suspect the truth either and was shocked by her abrupt departure, says a disbelieving Kelly, who hints she may have had her hand in the register to help support her habit.

"I called in and quit over the phone. Toward the end I was beginning to call in sick or come in late, but they loved me. They truly believed that I 'went weird' from the car accident."

Now alone in her condo with nothing else to distract her, she spent her entire day snorting cocaine and drinking. Her alcohol consumption by this time had reached a half-gallon a day.

"That's when it all escalated and plunged me to the depths. I isolated myself in my condo. I did cocaine in the morning and then drank alcohol to try and calm down. But I had to be careful not to drink too much, or I'd black out and then eat everything in the house. I wouldn't go anywhere without cocaine.

"I sold a home I owned and was renting out for rock bottom money. I lost money on it just to get the cash out. I used my savings and the pension I received when I left my job. I literally lost everything—my condo, my house, and my Mercedes, which went back to the bank. When I did go into treatment, I had a Mustang and myself."

Eventually, Kelly asked her brother, Scott, to move in with her to stand between her and using. "During the last three months I used, I knew I had to give it up. So I asked my brother if he'd move in and be my bodyguard. I didn't tell him I was using cocaine, but I admitted about the alcohol. I told him I'd pay for his school or whatever he needed.

"The day he moved in, I knew I had made a mistake because now I knew I couldn't stop. He put me on a drug and alcohol diet, and I started sneaking around behind his back. He thought he could help me, but he couldn't. He said, 'I don't know what we should do, but I can't handle this, and you need help.' I said, 'No, I've changed my mind. You don't live with me anymore.' I had admitted I had a problem, but the denial went back up so quickly."

It was also about this time that Kelly took a panicky drive to her sister's home more than 2½ hours away. "She lived 200 miles away from me, but I drove over to her house to give her all of my cocaine—vials of it. She knew I used, but she didn't know the extent of it.

"I remember sitting in her bathtub; I was all strung out, I weighed less than 100 pounds, and I remember how she looked at me. I said to her, 'You have to help me. Take these from me. I can't do it by myself.' She was shocked and said, 'Not in my house.' But she kept them. I got cleaned up and drove home.

"But as soon as I got to my house, I turned around and drove back and begged her for it. She said, 'Kelly, you don't know what you're doing.' I said, 'Just give it back to me, and I'll give it to someone else so I won't have to put you out.' Then I literally got into my car and did a line right there. I could barely make it to the car because I needed the coke so badly. It was like, 'Oh, what were you ever thinking that you have a problem?' But it was a real milestone for me. I knew the truth then." She cringes. "I have shivers right now, just talking about it."

Her sister Janet, now 35 and a nurse, was shocked by what she saw that night, and she didn't know how to handle Kelly or help her. "I didn't know anything about cocaine. She gave me five grams and told me to try to sell them for her. Our relationship wasn't very good, and I would have done anything to make it better; so I thought, 'Well, okay.'

"But she was so thin, like 90 pounds. She was also very hyper and short-tempered. She was sitting in my bathtub, and she was hysterical. I had to call in sick to stay home from work with her."

It was that night, Janet recalls, that Kelly introduced her to cocaine. Although she didn't like it initially, she also began to use it for weight control a year or two later and eventually developed a $100-a-week habit herself.

Says Janet, "I tried cocaine that night and thought, 'So what's the big deal?' Kelly insisted, 'Oh, it's just your first time. You've got to do it again.' I didn't do it again for a long time. But then I tried it again one night at a party a year or two later and suddenly found I wasn't hungry anymore. I guess what happened to Kelly didn't scare me enough, and I never knew she used it for weight control. I guess I just thought I could handle it."

Janet points out that until the last few years—although all three siblings suffered from both eating disorders and she and her sister from cocaine addiction as well—they each thought they were alone in their distress. "We just didn't see it," she shrugs.

Kelly continued to use and drink after that incident, and her brother finally moved out. But during the week she had left her live-in boyfriend, Kelly had met and begun dating a man she describes as a very successful business owner. And less than a year into their relationship, her brother requested this man's help.

"Toward the end my boyfriend had also become aware I had a problem because I would do very strange things," Kelly recalls. "I would say I'd be places and not show up. I'd come out of blackout with him. All of a sudden, he started to notice that I wasn't really all there. When my brother told him, 'This is what's happening with her' and brought it to his attention, he said, 'Now it all makes sense.' When you don't know that an illness exists, symptoms will not get through to you. And that's exactly what happened.

"My brother said, 'That's enough.' He took me over to this guy's house, and they gave me a choice of hospitals. I chose a 10-day program versus a 30-day program to get the cure rather than the lifelong program of recovery."

Though she was forced into treatment, Kelly recalls an overwhelming feeling of relief. "I was basically grateful because once I got there, they told me I was an alcoholic but that I didn't have to drink anymore. I said, 'Thank God. I now know what's wrong with me,' and they promised me the cure."

Kelly wanted to put her turmoil behind her, but she certainly didn't want to do it at the expense of gaining weight. She didn't admit to the doctors that she had an eating disorder or that she was using cocaine.

"I didn't know what an eating disorder was, but I did believe that if I didn't have cocaine, I'd get fat. I was willing to give up my addiction, but only if I didn't have to gain weight to do it. Plus, I felt it was a worse stigma to be a drug addict than it was to be an alcoholic. I took speed the day I got out."

Upon leaving the program, Kelly also decided to make an impulsive move to southern California, a place she had never even visited. It was, she explains, another escape mechanism. She says, "I had a vision that if I moved to California, I would be able to change my life. I moved the day I got out of rehab. I had no job, nothing. I had never even been there before. I called Century 21 and had a realtor meet me at the airport. She showed me around, and I said, 'Yup, this is where I want to be.' I got myself a condo. I thought, 'This will be the answer to my problems. I'll run on the beach, I'll get it together, and I'll never drink again.' But I didn't go to A.A."

Initially Kelly had enough money from property she had sold in Seattle and loans from friends, but soon she took a job as a salesclerk in a branch of the same store she had once helped manage up in Seattle. She spent three months without taking a drink, but she did use speed. Then she slipped up entirely.

"I never thought I'd drink again, but it was like picking up a cup of coffee, and it scared me. I was with some friends, and I had a margarita. They said, 'Kelly, we didn't know you drank.' I looked at them and said, 'Neither did I.' I was back into cocaine and everything else that night. For the next three weeks it was worse than it ever was."

This time Kelly went for help on her own. She desperately wanted to escape the insanity and was now willing to make the commitment to do it. At age 26 she made a final pledge to sobriety and a new lifestyle.

"This time nobody forced me. It was my own decision. I went to A.A., and I've been clean and sober since 1981. Because I drank again after my cure, I was willing to do whatever I had to do. I was petrified. I went to a meeting, got a sponsor, and did what I was told. I worked the 12 Steps of recovery and developed a lifestyle."

· Though she gave up both alcohol and cocaine through Alcoholics Anonymous at that time, it was another four months or so before she confessed to her eating disorder. "I knew something was wrong," she concedes, "but I didn't know it was an eating disorder and that other people suffered from the same malady. I would go to A.A. meetings and casually say, 'God, I've got to quit eating so much sugar,' but I wouldn't tell anyone how much I was really eating. They'd say, 'Oh, don't worry about it. You need sugar. Everybody needs sugar when they're coming off alcohol.' But I knew that I was different.

"One night I went out to dinner with some friends, and I heard this woman say she was a compulsive overeater. I had never heard the word before. She said she went to O.A. I asked very casually, not letting her know I might need it, 'What's O.A.?' I called her later and told her I needed help. She said, 'I understand' and took me to a meeting of Overeaters Anonymous."

O.A., according to Kelly, works on the same principles as other anonymous programs. "They follow the same 12-Step program, but they deal with food the way that alcoholics deal with alcohol or cocaine addicts deal with cocaine. At the Rader Institute we refer anyone with no funds or insurance to O.A. It's a great program."

Today Kelly's eating disorder is as much under control as her alcoholism and addiction. "I don't control it, but it is under control," she philosophizes about her situation. "I work the program, and I'm better off than most of the population. I eat healthy food, I don't worry about my weight, and I don't have a problem. I don't have to diet.

"When I do have thoughts about using food, I know that there are things in my life that need my attention, and I have to check it out. I use it as a barometer to go forward. It's one day at a time."

Both her siblings have also conquered their eating disorders. Kelly's brother, who admitted he was bulimic to her when she first entered treatment, found religion in his college years and arrested his eating disorder without counseling. In 1987 Janet shocked Kelly, despite her own history, with her admissions that she was bulimic, an alcoholic, and addicted to marijuana and cocaine.

Kelly had begun counseling other people with eating disorders shortly after her own recovery and by 1984 was an intervention counselor at The Rader Institute. She encouraged Janet to enter the program there.

Today Kelly recognizes the progression of her eating disorder into addiction as a rather likely one. "They're two separate diseases, but they're both related to physical and mental obsession. Self-esteem is the root of it all, but it's a real phenomenon. I think some of it is genetics, some is environmental, and some is attributable to the fact that if you drink or use enough drugs, you can create an addiction. But it's very real. Once you take your first bite or that first drink, you cannot control what will happen."

She finds particular satisfaction in helping others escape the torment she suffered for so many years. "I work with the families and help them break the denial so they can ask for help, and I know this is what I'm supposed to be doing with my life," she explains. "It's very fulfilling." The most important advice she offers to family and friends is to interfere with an addict's self-destructive behavior no matter what the consequences.

"When I got sober, everyone said, 'God, I'm so glad,' but no one had ever interceded except for my brother at the very end. They'd all known, but no one ever said anything to me. They definitely should have, and I hope that's the message I carry now: risk anger, risk everything, but confront them."

Not only have Kelly's experiences made her professional life exceptional, her personal life has come full circle as well.

"My life today is great. I've been happily married since 1985 to a man who owns a health center. He's wonderful, and I'm very lucky. I believe that I had to go through all that then in order to find this now. I have to believe that—it's the spiritual aspect of my program. Even when I get addled today, I feel my experiences are just meant to take me on from here."

SANDIE

STRIPPER, PROSTITUTE, AND MOTHER
LOS ANGELES, CALIFORNIA

Sandie, always a rebellious youth, ran away from a middle-class home at age nine, when her mother was divorcing her second husband, Sandie's adoptive father. Although she drifted in and out of her parents' homes until age 14, she basically lived on the streets for the next 15 years. Already an alcohol and marijuana user, she was introduced to cocaine at age 16 and began a heavy love affair with the drug. In her late teens, to better support her habit, she worked as a nude dancer and a prostitute. At the height of her addiction, 'basing as much as half an ounce a day, Sandie says, "God blessed me." A man she approached on the boulevard as a trick was intrigued by her, got her off the street, and eventually helped her kick her habit. She became pregnant by him on their first encounter and went to live with him. Though she continued to use drugs during her pregnancy and the couple temporarily lost custody of their newborn twins as a result, today Sandie has been sober almost a year and a half and is raising two healthy and very active toddlers. Recently, at age 25, she married the man who saw something special and fell in love with her, the man she credits with saving her life.

"If you see my situation, maybe you can understand my destination" is the final haunting line of a poem written by Sandie as a teenager living on the streets. Nicknamed Breeze "because I never stayed in one place too long," Sandie plans to publish her collection of poems someday under that winsome moniker. Today Sandie has many dreams that only a few years ago, in the midst of her cocaine addiction, seemed entirely unattainable.

"As a matter of fact, I have a poem that talks about my story being a number-one best-seller," she muses. "Even though I was getting high and basically living on the street, I still knew where I was going. I was very creative."

While Sandie was unusual in the fact that she persisted in her zeal for living, the reality of her existence on the streets was much more stark.

"I guess I was pretty much a problem child. I don't know why. I was the middle child. I had an older sister who was an angel and a younger brother who's spoiled rotten to this day. So in order to get any attention from my folks, I had to be the exact opposite. I had to be recognized.

"I was about nine years old, and I was unhappy at home. I'm really an independent individual, and I didn't like the rules. Also, the marriage was unhappy, and my parents were divorcing. I just didn't want to be there. I went in and out of the house, but the last time I really lived at home, I was 14, and that was for a month.

"I basically slept on the street. It was definitely terrifying, but it was either live by myself or live with the rules. I'd say it was normal reprimanding, not abusive, but I couldn't handle the rules."

Sandie's father was a real-estate agent, and her mother worked first as a cosmetologist and later as a waitress. There was no history of substance abuse in her family, but as Sandie explains, drugs are just a fact of life on the streets.

"I wasn't looking for drugs; it was just the thing. Peer pressure, I guess. I was wild and crazy. After pot and drinking came cocaine, and you learn to love it, that's for sure. I don't remember who introduced me to it, probably a boyfriend.

"At age 15 I started freebasing. I was into keg parties—kegs of beer and local bands at backyard parties. Then the parties became more classy, so to speak. That's a real false term, but it's used in drug life. It was etiquette to go to a real nice home. People with money have cocaine. That's why I became a prostitute. If I had money, I had cocaine."

Though Sandie didn't actually begin walking the streets until her late teens, she learned quite early that sexual favors, while not performed for money, got her other things she needed and wanted. "I remember having to sleep with people, having to give up my body for a warm place to sleep and something to eat. I had sex by the time I was 10, not really by choice, but basically to survive. I don't know how I came to know my body could get me things. I just somehow knew that if I let a man kiss me, touch me, etc., etc., etc., I could probably spend the night inside, warm. I learned to use sex to get what I wanted.

"There were a few boyfriends I can really say I cared for and for whom drugs didn't play a big part in our relationship. But I think I was with those men more as father figures. That's really why I lasted with a man. I needed security."

Sandie loved cocaine for its ability to mask her emotions as much as for the euphoric high it provided. There's a great deal of her childhood that she can't recall, a casualty of both drug use and emotional shutdown.

"There's a lot of that part of my life I don't really remember. I think it's because I was on so many drugs. You just can't function. And there's definite emotional shutdown. There were a lot of things I didn't want to deal with—rejection from my mom, not feeling loved, not feeling all kinds of things. Not feeling a part of anything really, not even my own life.

"Coke made all the problems go away. You didn't have to feel the emotions; it masks anything you seriously have to deal with in your life that hurts. Or maybe even anything that feels good if you're not ready to feel it. You use something to take away those feelings, and that's cocaine.

"There was the euphoria too. That's what you search for from day one. You're continually trying to get as high as you did on that initial high. As most cocaine addicts will say, freebasing is like 1,000 orgasms in one."

Cocaine also made a very lost little girl feel very grown up. "I was big and I was important because I did cocaine. I had it totally together because I did cocaine. And with snorting it's really more the act of doing it that's the exciting part, that attracts people. You put it on a mirror, and a mirror's neat. It reflects light and the razor blade, and you make designs with the coke. But then your life becomes like a broken mirror."

Though she was living on the streets, Sandie continued to attend school, at least semiregularly. Although she never graduated, she did learn to read and write.

"I made it pretty much to the ninth grade, but I'm an exception to the rule. I did a lot of things differently. I don't even know how I made it. Like I said, there are things I just plain don't remember."

Despite what was going on in her life, no one at school seemed to suspect Sandie's plight. "There were 32 kids in a class," shrugs Sandie, who always takes responsibility for her own destiny. "How could they pay attention to just me? I do remember one teacher trying to get involved, trying to help the relationship between me and my mother. But it didn't work out."

At age 15 Sandie was arrested for the first time for grand theft auto. She was, she insists indignantly, falsely accused. "I was set up! I was so innocent about it. I was 15 and living on a nude beach. We borrowed a car from a fellow beachgoer and went to the store. By the time we got back, the girl had left with another chick, someone to make money from. Rather than leave the car at the beach, where we knew a lot of cars left overnight are vandalized, we took it into Hollywood and spent the night at a friend's house.

"This girl lived with her folks, who didn't know she was a drug addict and prostitute. Her father had told her if she ever lent the car to anyone, he would take it away. The next day, when she couldn't explain where her car was, she lied and said that it was stolen."

Though Sandie was too young to drive and her boyfriend was actually piloting the car, she says ruefully, "I took the rap because I didn't want my boyfriend to go to prison."

Her parents wanted nothing more to do with her. Sandie became a ward of the court and was sentenced to juvenile hall for five months. While locked up, she suffered a tubular pregnancy that nearly killed her. In fact, she claims, she had a near-death experience.

"I called my parents, and they wouldn't come get me. My mom had just had enough. 'No, I won't come get you, sorry.' I was pretty darn depressed.

"I had a tubular pregnancy. I was sick, but they didn't believe me. They told me all I wanted to do was escape. They treated me pretty badly. I was basically dying, and all they would give me was Tylenol. I had terrible stomach cramps, and they thought I was constipated.

They gave me eight enemas. I'd sit on the toilet in my room and scream, and they'd just bang on the door and tell me to shut up.

"Then I just collapsed on the way back from eating. They took me down to the infirmary and rushed me to the hospital. They put this needle way up in me and said, 'Oh, my God, get this woman to surgery.' Boom, it was done. I had 4½ pints of blood in my stomach. I was almost five months pregnant.

"But I did die. I saw life after death. I saw the light, the tunnel. I spoke with Jesus and the Mother Mary."

Shortly thereafter, Sandie took off cross-country, the first of four trips, hitchhiking with truckers and scoring drugs where she could. Overall, she looks back on it as a good experience, but she realizes how lucky she is to have survived and recalls one harrowing experience.

"One time, when I was 16, I was traveling with a man who was about 22. We got picked up by a trucker. The man I was with had to boost me up into the truck, and there was a gun pointed at my head. The driver asked, 'Do you have a weapon?' I've got a really outgoing attitude, and I told him, 'Of course I have a weapon—for idiots like you.' This man put his gun down and said, 'Good, because you know what? If you had put yourself in a position like that, hitchhiking out in the middle of nowhere, I'd have shot you because you were so stupid.' I ended up traveling across the state of Texas with the man. We all actually got pretty friendly."

Her roving didn't slow down her drug abuse, and Sandie either bought drugs or received them as a gift. "I'd find somebody to give me a bag of weed or this, that, or the other thing. I traded sex. You know the old saying—a friend with weed is a friend indeed. And I bought it off the street. I'm sure I've worked in every fast-food chain there is. Then I got false I.D. and worked as a cocktail waitress."

Once, while on the road, Sandie attempted to re-establish contact with her family. But again, her mother rebuffed her effort.

"I called my mother from Louisiana one time. She asked, 'Why did you call me?' I said, 'Because I missed you,' and she replied, 'Please don't call and upset me. Don't tell me my daughter's in some truck stop.' "

Sandie did maintain some contact with her father, to whom she felt she could "tell anything." She didn't get along with her father's new wife, however, and ultimately, he wasn't much help either. But he did once save her from a suicide attempt in her mid-teens.

"I attempted suicide three times. I don't remember how old I was, but one time, in my boyfriend's apartment, I sliced my arms from the wrists to my elbows from every different angle you could possibly do it. Then I put my hands in the toilet and flushed, which sucked the blood out. I passed out, and the next thing I knew, the fire department was busting down the door to the bathroom. I don't even know how in the hell he found out, but my dad was there.

"I could tell my father almost anything. He gave me money when I needed it to buy clothes and stuff like that. He tried to help me, but his wife and I didn't get along; so living in his house didn't work. I'm sure it broke his heart, but he told me, 'Well, honey, you've got to do what you've got to do.' He just said, 'Look, I thought I taught you better than that, but you're in it, and I can't do anything about it. You're your own person. I'm not going to lock you in the house and tie you down.' "

When her travels ended and Sandie returned to Los Angeles again, she attempted to establish some semblance of normality in her life. She landed a job as a nurse's assistant in a convalescent nursing home. She took classes at lunchtime and actually obtained her certification as a licensed vocational nurse. She maintained for two years.

"Instead of somebody taking care of me, I was trying to take care of somebody else. I thought it would make me feel better about taking care of myself. When I was nursing, I wasn't really that into cocaine. I didn't use while I was working, just at night. I snorted a quarter gram on the weekends or something like that. But I didn't like the way the home was run, how the patients were treated, so I left. After I left, I became more involved with coke."

To make more money, Sandie began working as a nude dancer in a downtown Hollywood nightclub. The availability of cocaine in that atmosphere quickly escalated her developing addiction.

"I was 18. I was living in and out of motels a lot. I never really had a home, not for any length of time greater than six months to a year. I mostly stayed with friends. I'm a great dancer, and I have a great body; so I became a dancer, a stripper.

"I made a lot of money. I also had as many drug tips as money. Your regular customers, who are in the bar every night, come and tip you $20 and a quarter gram of cocaine. Or they give you a couple of lines here, a couple of lines there or buy you a drink. I made $300 to $500 a night, plus drugs. But I also bought drugs out of my own money." In that atmosphere Sandie's drug use escalated quickly. She soon ravaged her nose with a two-gram-a-day habit and switched to freebasing.

"Somehow cocaine and I mixed. I definitely functioned well. I snorted a long time until it just burnt me out and wasn't enough anymore. I just depleted my nose. It felt like I destroyed all the cartilage, and I just couldn't snort anymore. I was blowing my nose and sniffing constantly or just rubbing the end. It was ridiculous. But it really got out of hand when I started freebasing. Eventually I would use a quarter to half an ounce a day smoking."

While dancing, Sandie became pregnant by a man she was dating. Although she obtained some prenatal care, she continued freebasing, though not heavily. On March 17, 1986, she gave birth to a healthy baby girl. Sandie then broke up with her boyfriend, also a heavy user, in an attempt to clean up. She stopped using and rented a house.

"I had a real bad habit, but I did have some control. I knew that if I had a chance by myself with her, I could've done it. I would have taken care of her and quit doing drugs. I had a house, but I had to go back to work for both of us to survive.

"The baby's father didn't like the fact that I was dancing, and he was very jealous that I was trying to stop using. I had been sober for about two months. But he came back, and love hit me again. He helped me screw up, though it was my own decision. I fought with him, and he kidnapped her.

"It hurt me so much what this man was doing to me. After all, I had tried to get him sober, and I had been sober for a while. I couldn't really support myself in a legitimate job at that point; I was a dancer. So I couldn't prove myself to be a fit mother. A month later he gave the baby to a girlfriend of mine, who became licensed foster care through the courts. She fought for and kept my baby, now she's adopted her. I gave my baby up for cocaine, but I still see her."

For Sandie, who had wanted a child desperately, losing her 3-month-old baby drove her to total despair and complete abandon in her drug abuse.

"She was my firstborn, and I've had four miscarriages and one tubular pregnancy. I had it pretty tough trying to have a child. Then to have one taken from me. After I lost her, I really got into coke. For two years I just didn't care.

Sandie left dancing to pursue prostitution full time. It was, she realized, both good money and less work, although she did find it to be more dangerous.

"I'm lucky I'm alive," she realizes. "I was raped three times. That was pretty tough. One trick held a knife to my throat and actually cut me. I felt the blood dripping, and that was what really freaked me out. I thought, 'Oh, my God, am I going to live?' Then he warned me and left. Of course, I waited. He said he would come back and kill me if I didn't."

Sandie credits the bravado she's exhibited from a young age with helping her survive the streets. Once accosted by her pimp, she refused to associate with him anymore. "Once he slapped me across the face, but I'm so independent, he was just no longer my guard."

Sandie was picked up a number of times for prostitution and actually arrested three times, but only one arrest resulted in jail time. The treatment she encountered at the hands of the police, however, was almost more degrading than what she encountered on the street.

"Are you kidding me? There's terrible verbal abuse from police officers at the station when you're busted for prostitution. One time the cop who busted me had his hands between my legs. I asked him, 'How could you do that?' He said, 'Well, if you're going to treat yourself like shit.' It didn't give him the right, but it was true. I believe this guy was sorry he couldn't get it. If he wasn't actually on duty, he would have done it with me and paid for it too. Shows how good our cops are, because I have slept with off-duty police officers.

"I got hauled in a lot, but not arrested. They just want to find out who you are and then they let you go. I did 10 days in jail on one occasion, and it just wasn't a good experience. You have somebody sitting there watching you go to the bathroom in the morning. You have to roll cigarette tobacco in toilet tissue. You have no rights while you're there. It wasn't a pleasant place to be.

"I slept a lot and slept through meals. The withdrawal did hurt a little, and you don't feel like eating. Your stomach is wretched, like worn out. You keep saying, 'Oh, I wish I could quit, I wish I could quit,' but you get out and do it again.

"I don't know how I went so far. There were times I passed out and woke up with my pipe sitting in my lap. I must have totally exhausted my body. There are a couple of times I dropped a pipe and burnt myself. My body just couldn't take anymore, and I fell asleep."

Though she had a physically devastating drug habit and was walking the streets, Sandie was unusual in being very meticulous about her personal habits. In fact, the only health problem she ever encountered was an occasional nosebleed.

"The only reason I didn't overdose is because I ate and took care of my body—besides destroying it," she laughs. "People who O.D. don't eat for three days. They take a real good hit, their resistance is down, they're weak, and *boom*. Most people can't eat while they're on cocaine, but I could have my pipe on the table while I was eating a full-course meal. And I always made sure that I drank plenty of water.

"I didn't let myself go, and I kept clean. I said to many of my friends, 'God, why don't you take a shower and put some clean clothes on? You can still 'base afterwards; you'll probably enjoy the high better.'

"I had AIDS tests and all kinds of tests throughout my prostitution history—in case a rubber broke or something. I was definitely up on myself and survival. Although I had a real bad habit, it just didn't affect me like it does a lot of people. I took care of myself real well."

One night Sandie was walking on Sunset Boulevard, a notorious area for prostitution in L.A. She approached a car looking for a trick and encountered the man who would become her husband. It was, they claim, practically love at first sight.

"I was freebasing anywhere from three to five grams a day. I was dealing cocaine to support my habit and prostituting. I propositioned my last 'date'—although I didn't know that then. He didn't even know what I was doing. I told him what it would cost him, and he said, 'Thirty dollars, are you kidding me?' And that was just for a ride around the block! But he was so attracted to me. He wanted to be with me no matter what.

"When I got into the car, he was just too friendly to be a trick. He wasn't one, and I didn't treat him like one. I liked the way he looked, and I just wanted to be in his car."

Peter, now 29, worked both then and now as a painting contractor. A Hungarian immigrant, he has a heavy accent. He was able, he explains, to look beyond the prostitution and the drug abuse and see a beautiful human being.

"I was a little bit shocked," he recalls. "I was just a regular person. I had never lived a wild life like Sandie. But she was just so happy about everything. She had so much life in herself. When she wasn't high on coke, we talked about life, and she showed me herself. There was a whole different person underneath all the bullshit of drugs. She has a beautiful mind. I tried to help her, tried to get her off drugs. That's how I fell in love with her. Two weeks later she moved in with me."

Sandie, who scrupulously used birth control, didn't that night, and she later found out she was pregnant with his children—twins. "I always used birth control except for that night. It was like, 'I don't know who you are, man, but you are an angel sent from I-don't-know-where.'

"I was so happy when this man fell in love with me. I thought, 'Finally, a man to really give me what I need.' And that just meant someone to be there for me, no matter what. He liked me so much, he said he would pay me anything to not go out on the street again. I quit the day I met him, gladly. I think I told him I loved him a week after we met.

"But I couldn't just disappear. I had to get out of that life. I had dating and escort services and two or three pimps. It was two weeks later when I moved in with him and out of my motel."

"That was the deal," Peter details. "She moved in, and she stopped doing drugs. She did okay for a week, but then she had a craving, and she started to do it again."

Since Sandie was no longer walking the streets, the twosome began dealing to support her habit. Peter quit his work, although he himself never used. "I didn't know how to help her in another way. I was hoping something would come up, that it would change somehow. That's why I supported her habit—because she wouldn't stop, and she would just have gone somewhere else to get it. She said that even though she loved me, she had to have it, and if I didn't help her, she would go and get it somewhere else. She might have ended up prostituting herself. I didn't want her to go and do stupid things for the drugs when she wasn't really wanting to do that. I was already in love with her. That's why it was hard to do anything stronger."

"He never used; I just introduced him to dealing it," Sandie confesses. "He loved me so much that he would do anything to have me
there. He's a very sensitive, gentle, passive person, and I basically
bossed him around to get what I wanted. I forced him to put our
jewelry in pawnshops. I forced him to do a lot. He definitely adopted
my lifestyle out of love. He thought it was something that would pass,
and he'd just have to deal with it.

"But we fought. He'd tell me, 'This shit's got to stop, Sandie,' and
I'd threaten him. I'd say, 'Fuck you. I'll go get it somewhere else.'
There were plenty of times that he walked out because he hated the
way I looked.

"Twice I waved a gun at him because I was hallucinating. We had a
lot of gold and money in the house because we were dealing, and I
thought there were intruders. I didn't shoot it, but I hit the wall with
it and left holes. I screamed at him, 'Do you want to feel it or see it?'
meaning did he want me to shoot him or watch me shoot myself?"

As her pregnancy became obvious, Peter pressured her even harder
to give up drugs.

"I tried to tell her, but she didn't want to understand anything. It
was pretty tough. I didn't know how to help her get out from the
thing."

"I already had a habit when I became pregnant, and oh, well, . . . in
my mind, I always said, 'Well, I'm just preparing them for what life is
really about. The air we breathe isn't much better—with cigarette
smoke and all,' " Sandie philosophizes.

"I think attitude has a lot to do with it. If I had sat there rubbing
my stomach saying, 'Oh, I'm so sorry I'm doing this to you,' if I had
been down on myself for it, it probably would have affected my kids
more. But I always had the attitude that 'They're fine. I'm eating, I'm
sleeping, they're fine.'

"Today, I feel so strongly, if I saw a pregnant woman with a 'base
pipe in her mouth, I'd probably knock her out."

To avoid detection of her drug use, Sandie didn't seek out prenatal
care. Still, she had very definite ideas on child care. "I made three
visits to the doctor, at three different stages of the pregnancy. The
first time I went just to verify it. The second time, I wanted to know
how far along I was. He just did a vaginal exam. I wouldn't allow
him to do ultrasound, because I don't believe in it. If there's no prob-

lem with a pregnancy, I don't think you should put sound waves through your baby. I was pretty much into the au naturel."

Eventually, Sandie and Peter were busted for dealing coke; however, only Peter was actually prosecuted. He spent four days in jail.

"It was terrible," he emphasizes. "I didn't understand what was happening. They didn't let me shower for four days—and no cigarettes. At that time I was smoking two packs of cigarettes a day; so it was very bad. I felt bad about myself, too, for what I had done. But it was already done; so I was just waiting to see what was going to happen. The kids weren't born yet; it was heartbreaking. I was losing everything."

When he was finally released, Sandie recalls, "He looked like hell. He hadn't showered. He hadn't shaved. He hadn't brushed his teeth. It was terrible."

But despite what her drug use was doing to her relationship with the man she loved, Sandie continued to use. "I knew the last time that I freebased, December 17, 1987, and my kids were due any minute, that it would be the last time.

"I went to a county hospital because I thought it would be pretty loose. But it turns out they check. Almost all hospitals automatically take urine and blood tests. They discovered the children had cocaine in their systems. The doctors contacted social workers, and I couldn't take my babies home."

"Middle-class mothers are usually able to escape detection in the hospital when they give birth," explains Stephen Ambrose, director of the New Beginnings Project at the Los Angeles Children's Institute, where Sandie now attends a counseling program for parents. "When women go to a private hospital, they're paying money for privacy, and they get privacy. But the protocol is much more stringent at county hospitals. Any mother who has not had prenatal care is at high risk of drug involvement."

The children, Sandie claims, were born with no apparent symptoms of withdrawal from the drug usage. "I'm real fortunate. My kids, a boy and a girl, didn't have symptoms at all, nothing. I'm just plain blessed. With so many people I know, their kids have seizures and this, that, and the other.

"But birth problems are related more to living style than actual drug use. Like I said, I ate every day. Doctors will tell you there are no long-term physical effects from cocaine use, but I do think there are some emotional effects.

"I believe that my son had a few of the emotional effects of withdrawal. He had to be held a little bit more. But I'm making assumptions. Maybe my son's just a loving person and needs to be cuddled more. There are babies like that who never had any exposure to cocaine."

"When we first saw Sandie's babies, they had already been returned to her, and at that point there were no dramatic signs of withdrawal," Ambrose confirms. "She denies that there were any right after they were born. That may or may not be true. Most mothers don't want to recognize a baby's symptoms from having been exposed to drugs. They feel guilty; so they'll blind themselves to the damage done.

"But these two kids really do seem to be doing well. I think Sandie's done a pretty good job of parenting them. And there is an interactive question. Letting a child go through foster-home experiences, one after another, can be more damaging in the long haul than the drug exposure. But the two causes are often confused.

"The other things that go along with drug use are poor nutrition or exposure to diseases that can worsen the situation. Maybe she was able to maintain adequate nutrition and wasn't exposed to any venereal diseases or hepatitis or AIDS. And there may be differences in the way the fetus handles the drug or in the extent of the drug exposure and the timing of it—in what trimester.

"But it's very hard to diagnose, and while there may be no immediate withdrawal symptoms, people are beginning to be concerned that there may be long-term learning and emotional disabilities."

Because of Peter's drug arrest, he was also unable to gain custody of their children, and the twins were awarded to foster care. Losing the babies, however, was enough to make Sandie finally take stock of her life and decide to sober up.

"I thought, 'This is it; it's time to get real.' I just made the decision to totally clean my life up. It hurt me so bad when I lost my first baby. That just killed me, and I couldn't lose these two. Cocaine had finally taken something important from me."

The day after Sandie got out of the hospital she went to court to establish her interest in regaining custody of the children. On a lawyer's advice she went to a community counseling program and immediately got on a program of random drug testing. She also made rapid contact with the foster family to obtain visiting rights.

"I called the home and asked to see the children. When I came, they heard my story and saw the bonding between me and my kids.

"Once a week I went to counseling, sometimes twice if I felt I needed it. Surprisingly enough, I was so open and honest with my counselor. I was ready to stop, and I told her everything. I'd call and tell her, 'I had a dream last night, and I'm scared to death I'm going to use,' and she'd tell me to come over.

"You wake up in a cold sweat from a dream about having a pipe in your mouth and taking a hit. You wake up and say, 'Oh, my God, it couldn't be. Please don't tell me I did it.' You wake up and actually think you feel the high. That's what they call a dry high. You actually feel the rush. And it's not a good feeling at all, because then you feel like you failed.

"It's a real hard thing to deal with—all the cravings. You have no patience level, and you just snap instantaneously. One wrong word and it's, 'I hate you! Get out of my face! Shut up! Don't talk to me!' I was real irritable, I couldn't sleep, and I had a lack of comprehension."

But Sandie persevered, and a month later she regained custody of her babies. Her children are now a year-and-a-half old, but she continues to attend the parenting classes taught by Ambrose.

"One of the conditions for the children to be returned to Sandie was that she enroll in our parenting program," he explains. "She's been fortunate. It concerns me how decisions are made about if and when babies should be returned to parents. It's real arbitrary. Many mothers in her circumstances would have had a different social worker or judge, and it wouldn't have happened that way. She would have had to jump through a million hoops to get her babies back. Other mothers who are far more dysfunctional than Sandie may have their babies returned to them directly from the hospital."

Sandie advocates the support program for any prospective parent—male or female, drug abuser or not. "It's extremely important," she enthuses. "What it does is give you alternative ways of thinking. Like they'll tell you, 'How about taking time out instead of smacking the kids on the hand?' And you think, 'Hey, that's really nice.'

Sandie feels her mothering instincts came naturally, and she has been able to forgive her own mother for her lack of parenting skills. Today they have re-established their relationship.

"I received counseling for the first year of my sobriety. I needed that. I broke down like a 3-year-old child and cried in my psychologist's arms. I've always had this instinct to mother. A lot of women are like that. But parenting skills were not there for my mom. She didn't know how to react to all the bad things I did. I had to learn to accept the fact that she didn't know what else to do."

Sandie, who believes her thinking won't be normalized for years to come, feels she hurt Peter more than she did herself, although he claims it was all worth it.

"Our babies are beautiful—they're just perfection," Peter boasts. "She stopped, and no more problems. She's a better person today, totally different. She loves her babies very much. She could not be any more."

"I think co-dependents suffer more than the dependents," Sandie says guiltily. "I know I hurt that man incredibly. But we have a great relationship today. He is fantastic. He's God's blessing to me, I'll tell you that. I love him so-o-o much. I am so-o-o happy. Sometimes I say to him, 'Aren't you glad I don't do that anymore?' And he says, 'Are you kidding? God, I love you so much.'

"But I also had to learn to take someone else's feelings into consideration. That's real different because all I've ever known is taking care of me. Now I need to take care of me so I can take care of him so he can take care of me."

Sandie has no regrets about the past, just plenty of enthusiasm and plans for the future. "The worst part was the rejection," she says thoughtfully. "People who haven't been there, who don't know anything about what people go through on the street, just don't want to know. It's the furthest thing from their perceptions. It's how people view you. I like to be viewed pleasantly, I suppose. Everybody does, you know?

"But I don't regret it at all. I don't regret anything in life, doing cocaine or anything. Because it all gave me experiences to grow from. Eventually it put me down, but it really helped me to see.

"I can still honestly say today that I love cocaine. I loved what it did for me, but I'm sure glad I don't use it. I couldn't. If I ever used it again, I'd die because I'd have to have it all.

"I would love to dance, just like Shirley MacLaine or Ginger Rogers. I want to publish my poetry under my nickname, Breeze. I'd still like to be a nurse. I want to be real involved in my kids' lives. And I'd like to be a drug and alcohol counselor, speaking at schools to kids even younger than junior high.

"I'd like to get hold of them before anything happens, let them know how rough it really is and how easy it is to get caught up in. Because it's nothing. It's just a snap away.

"I'm one of the lucky ones who should tell people just how lucky they are. God finally blessed me. He said, 'Okay, you've paid enough dues. Here you go, be happy.'"

TRACY

LICENSED PRACTICAL NURSE
DENVER, COLORADO

Tracy was 32 and working as a nurse in a Denver, Colorado, hospital when her addiction to cocaine and other drugs reached a crisis point. She refused to admit she was an addict who was not only killing herself, but endangering her patients. After being confronted by her nursing supervisor over missing drug supplies and humiliated by being arrested in front of her co-workers, she began the battle to kick a six-year addiction. Tracy was an only child, and her parents, fundamentalist Christians who doted on her, claim she ruined their lives as well as her own. Straight since 1983, Tracy has returned to nursing but admits her sobriety is a daily battle. Tracy and her parents tell her story from two entirely different viewpoints.

"I was such a good kid," recalls Tracy, now 37, "I didn't drink or do drugs. I didn't do *anything* wrong." By the time she tried cocaine, to which she quickly became addicted, she was in her late 20s and had already chosen and entered a "good girl" profession. She was a registered nurse working in a high-risk obstetrics ward in a Denver hospital.

Tracy, who is a lesbian, was introduced to cocaine by a female companion with whom she was "just totally head over heels in love." The woman, an aspiring artist who was frequently low on cash, dealt drugs—primarily cocaine—to supplement her income. So drugs were readily available.

Tracy's introduction to cocaine was unusual in that she was exposed to drug use by another woman. Most women are introduced by men, whether it's on a date or via a platonic friendship. But according to Tracy, there weren't really any male/female distinctions in the group she was using with. "I mainly hang around with women," Tracy explains, "but the people we used to shoot with were women and men. It wasn't gay or straight. It was just other people who did drugs."

The other unusual aspect of Tracy's drug use was that her introductory experience with cocaine was through a needle. Most addicts initially ingest cocaine through snorting. Only after the addiction has progressed do addicts generally turn to other methods, seeking an even better high—a high that matches the intensity of their first experience with cocaine.

"I think I had probably snorted cocaine a couple of times, but it really didn't do anything. It didn't affect me," says Tracy, who had had some experience smoking pot prior to that. Today she finds the progression of her drug use difficult to recall. "But then this woman I was in love with was doing it, and they introduced me to using needles, shooting it.

"I just happened to be hanging around, and being a nurse, I was appalled at their technique. They were reusing needles and everything. I thought, 'God, if you're going to do this, at least let me supply you with clean needles,' because at the time hepatitis was a big concern.

"So I was the person who supplied them with needles, and I would shoot people, put it into their veins. They all seemed to be having such fun that I tried it once, and that was it. I just loved it."

Tracy can't quite explain how, as a licensed practical nurse, she was able to ignore her medical training, overlooking the dangers of recreational drug use and the potential of addiction. "It's kind of hard to figure out why you do what you do," she shrugs. "I had a lot of problems with my parents, who were very unhappy I had chosen a gay lifestyle. I have a very low self-image, and shooting cocaine really helped me with that.

"Also, I didn't think I could become addicted, because I was a nice person. Nice people don't become addicted, and nurses help people. I was well liked at work, and I was a good nurse. For a long time I was able to continue being a nurse. I thought that what I did on my own time was my own business. You think you're not affected, but it fools you. You are.

"Also, little was known about cocaine at the time. They said it wasn't physically addictive, just psychologically."

Tracy also feels that her strict Christian upbringing and her parents' strenuous objections to her gay lifestyle encouraged her to go into a full-scale rebellion, albeit a little late in life. Part of the attraction to cocaine was the "naughtiness" of it.

"I don't know why, but being such a nice kid growing up, I sort of enjoyed sitting in a bathroom doing cocaine, thinking, 'God, if only these people knew what we were doing.'

"I also found out later that one of the problems was shooting. The needle really scares a lot of people, even men and women who snort cocaine. Maybe that was part of the attraction to it. I liked shooting it, the whole ritual—putting it on the spoon, mixing it, the instantaneous rush, the high, and the whole works. That was really attractive to me."

Tracy knew she was on a crash course and was able to give up drugs for a short period of time, but when she broke off her relationship with the woman who had introduced her to cocaine, she began shooting again, using the drug as an emotional crutch to boost her self-esteem.

"When I started up again, I really changed my way of doing it. I was very alone, and it became like a little ritual," says Tracy, whose addiction progressed quickly from there. "I ruined my life because of my ex-lover, but I don't blame anyone but me. No one forced me to stick a needle in my arm."

Eventually, Tracy used her entire savings account to buy cocaine, and her salary was inadequate to support her habit. She then began stealing drugs from the hospital to substitute for the cocaine.

"When you're shooting cocaine, you could go nonstop for days. If I had a few days off, that was all I did—no sleep, no nothing. Just stick the needle up your arm," she pauses morosely. "But coming down from cocaine is just the worst thing I've ever experienced in my life. It's horrible.

"Being a nurse, I went into different drugs to fulfill my needs. I found out that certain drugs—downers, Demerol in particular—helped me come down. So I began stealing. I was out of money, and essentially what I did was substitute what I got at work for free for cocaine."

At the height of her addiction Tracy was shooting several grams of cocaine a week, more if she could afford it. When that wasn't nearly enough, she began assuaging her cravings with Percodan and Demerol, as much as 500 milligrams a day, and heavy drinking. "That dosage would probably knock you on your rear. And, if I could get enough to do at work and bring some home, then I would. I also used to be able to pack away a lot of bourbon and Coke.

"I have a high tolerance anyway," Tracy adds. "Even when I go to the dentist and get a shot of Novocain, it takes like five shots and a long time to numb. Then, while I'm being worked on, I can still sort of feel it."

This fact may even have influenced the dramatic course of Tracy's addiction. According to the U.S. Department of Health and Human Services' Office for Substance Abuse Prevention, there is evidence that a high tolerance for intoxicating substances may predispose a person to addiction. This is due to the fact that a woman with a higher tolerance may not feel the same substance-induced effects as a woman with a lower tolerance, and she may use more to compensate.

Tracy relates that her addiction was further assisted by the ready availability of painkillers at the hospital. She worked in a high-risk obstetrics ward, where there were numerous cesarean sections and other surgical procedures.

"We gave a lot of Demerol and morphine; so if somebody was supposed to get a certain amount, I would sign out more and keep the rest for myself." Eventually, a patient who had only been at the hospital for 24 hours questioned her bill. Tracy had been the nurse attending the patient.

"She had gotten one 50-milligram shot of Demerol, and I had signed out 300 milligrams. By that time I was feeling really bad about what I was doing; so when I was confronted, I admitted my guilt. They called the police and everything, and I spent some time in jail."

Tracy actually spent only eight hours in jail, although it seemed an eternity. But as shameful as the experience was, being arrested at work and treated like a felon while in prison, it wasn't enough to make her quit doing drugs.

"I was totally humiliated. They had the vice squad at the hospital, and sitting in a jail cell, being treated like garbage by everyone, freaked me out. I was fingerprinted, they took my glasses away, and I couldn't see. But it obviously wasn't enough to affect me, because I started again."

Tracy has no idea how much she stole from the hospital, but the local paper, which reported her arrest, estimated the drugs at a street value of $10,000, all of which she took over a period of 5 to 6 months.

The staff at the hospital was incredibly supportive after she was released and given a second chance. "Everybody was very much behind me. When a lot of nurses go back, people aren't quite as understanding as the group I had. My nursing supervisor said, 'You're a good nurse. Go get some help, and we'll hire you back.'"

The help that was required by law included specialized counseling, regular urine tests, and court hearings to determine if she would be allowed to return to nursing. She was permitted to return, but the state nursing board had now placed her on probation, and the detection of any drug use in the future would result in the loss of her license to practice. She returned to work two months later with all good intentions.

"I got some help and started working back on the same floor and working graveyard again, which was really stupid. Working nights is boring and sort of conducive to doing drugs. That's when it finally dawned on me I had a drug problem. It hit me over the head like a hammer. I couldn't quit, and I was totally out of control."

She had been back at work four months and clean for six months when, unable to shake her addiction, she returned to her former behavior.

"It's taken a long time to look back, and sometimes I'm just really embarrassed at the way I behaved. They gave me a second chance, and I screwed it up. I felt very guilty for letting down the people who believed in me."

Being a nurse and having a good knowledge of physiology, Tracy was initially able to avoid detection of her relapse into drug use. But, "almost a year to the day," Tracy was caught a second time.

"I was lying to everyone, to myself, the therapist, and everyone. I even got away with giving urine tests. I worked nights, and what I would do, if I had to give urine the next day, is come home and drink gallons of water and jog about six miles to get my metabolism going and to flush out my system. Then I'd go in at the last possible minute to give my urine, and it would be clean. I got away with that for a few months.

"But it catches up. I was insane. I didn't sleep, because I spent all my time trying to clean out my system. I didn't have access to drugs, God forbid; so I was doing a lot of drinking, another substitute. Alcohol just never appealed to me until after the first time I got caught at work. I learned to like it.

"Not only that, but I would take or do anything. It wasn't social anymore. I had withdrawn. I didn't want to be with people; I wanted to be by myself."

Tracy feels she was "almost suicidal." It was during this time that she shot up one of her few remaining friends, and the woman almost died. It still wasn't enough to stop her.

"I shot a friend of mine with cocaine that happened to be a little more pure than what we were used to," Tracy shudders, "and I almost killed her. She quit breathing and turned blue and everything. Luckily, being a nurse and having taught CPR and all, I knew what to do.

"But then I started doing the same cocaine myself, even though I knew I could kill myself. And all the times I've been drunk, driving around . . . I just have an addictive personality."

Tracy was experiencing no noticeable health problems from her addiction; however, she did have several temporary reactions to her cocaine use. It was probably a nondrug substance used by the dealer to dilute the coke and increase the profits that landed her in the emergency room. Of course, she went to a hospital other than the one at which she worked.

"I don't think it was the cocaine. I think it was the cut. If it had been the cocaine, it would have probably killed me because of the amount I was doing. But my face puffed up. I told them I was using cocaine, and they looked at me like I was garbage. They gave me some medicine—because when you're using cocaine, you can quit breathing—kept me there awhile and then sent me home. And that was that."

Tracy's behavior on the job worsened, and so did her although they may have antidiscrimination statutes as broad as or broader than the federal law.

In summary, federal and state regulations may not directly forbid employers to ask specific questions of job applicants, and, in that sense, it may not be illegal to ask the questions. However, the regulations and guidelines consider many types of questions suspect. Such questions are presumed to be never done that before."

Tracy feels that she functioned fairly well on the job and that no one received inadequate care, but, she quickly adds, she really can't be sure. Her co-workers, she points out, never suspected a thing, even after her arrest.

"Looking back, I just don't know. I think I was always pretty much on top of it. Being so hyper, doing the drugs at work kind of calmed me down. There was one particular day—and I was doing everything then, shooting Demerol, taking Percodan—I had taken six Percodan in the space of eight hours. If there had been an emergency that night, I don't know if I could have responded appropriately. I remember feeling really out of it.

"But emergencies did happen, and I functioned fine. That was the thing that a lot of my co-workers had said, that they were *very* surprised. No one knew from my behavior."

"I worked with Tracy throughout the entire ordeal, and I'm still surprised," confirms former co-worker Pam, also a nurse, who remains her close friend today. "Everyone was shocked because she was an excellent nurse. She seemed very straight, not your 'typical' addict.

"I don't think it affected her job performance or her patient care until the very end, when she took some of the drugs prescribed for the patients. She tried so hard to cover up with the patients that it just didn't show. They got the best of her. She was kind and had a lot of patience. Even today patients come back and ask for her.

"But it did affect her relationship with her co-workers. She didn't have a lot of close friends. I was one of the very few. She was very hard to get along with, had no patience, and was irrational. She wouldn't try to work out a problem and had a short attention span. She's an only child, and we all thought she was just spoiled and immature.

"In retrospect, I guess there was some behavior that should have seemed abnormal. One time I approached her during the course of work, and she was very uneasy and frazzled. She was putting something in her purse. But when you're working alone at night, of course it's startling to have someone walk up behind you.

"She was also always very edgy, someone who just couldn't sit still or talk to you without playing with a pencil or looking around. But I had never known her any other way. It was easy to attribute her behavior to being a nervous kind of person. That's the biggest difference I see today. She's very relaxed."

In fact, when their nursing supervisor, tipped off by a night nurse who had noticed how much time Tracy was spending in the bathroom, found the caps from syringes in the wastebasket and confronted her, her co-workers were enraged.

"It was certainly a shock, even the second time it happened, when we should have all been looking for it," muses Pam about her naiveté. "But the second time around the administration watched her like a hawk; so I felt defensive and protective of her. Somehow, at the time it all seemed plausible. Nurses who are busy often drop used syringes in their pockets."

"I put on this little front, and I conned them," Tracy explains. "I was doing exactly what the head nurse had accused me of, but I was appalled that she even suspected me, and I strongly denied it. I had everyone behind me. They were all mad at the head nurse and said, 'Poor Tracy.' "

But Tracy's mother, Amy, saw a different side of the story and a decided change in her behavior. "I lost my real daughter. She was our whole life," she says, the bitterness apparent in her voice. "A beautiful girl, very smart and clean. We gave her piano lessons and skating lessons and sent her to college.

"And she turned into a pig. Not only was her appearance an embarrassment to me, her house was dirty and messy. I can't forget the time I called her in tears when her Dad had to be taken to the hospital emergency room. She didn't even show up to see him, and I was all alone.

"But I had no idea it was drugs. I blamed it all on her [gay] lifestyle. I just thought that's the way these kinds of girls do. I had to watch someone I loved ruin her life. We didn't even know where she was for over two years. She gave up her church, her true friends she grew up with, even her parents. I heard excuses, lies, and more lies."

Finally, Tracy gave a "dirty" urine, showing drug use. She was fired immediately and instantaneously lost her nursing license. It was, she claims, a relief.

"You know, I almost didn't care. I think, in a way, I was sort of glad. I knew that I needed to be away from nursing because I was just totally out of control. I would have done anything.

"But," she adds, thoughtfully, "it's devastating to anyone to lose a job, and it's particularly so to nurses because usually all nurses know is nursing. And even the addict on the street, so to speak, kind of looks down on a nurse who does drugs. 'You're a nurse! How could you do that?' "

Tracy's career was in ruins, and so were her finances and her relationship with her parents. Only recently she had bought a new house by enlisting her father as a cosigner for the loan. But now the property was in foreclosure, and she had to go live with her family.

"Nurses make fairly good money, and I was always proud that I could take care of myself. But now I had to go home to Mommy and Daddy, and that was really hard for me.

"I put them through a lot, and we still have our moments, but they have seen me change and become sober. So they're real supportive. But the people I affected most were my parents. I essentially killed them. They almost got a divorce over me. And my mom, more than my dad, still has a lot of anger.

"I can understand that—when you've lied and screwed up someone's life by putting them through this. But I get a little depressed because if I don't call regularly or seemingly fall into the pattern, she thinks I'm getting back into the drug use. Plus being gay. My parents are really religious. It takes a long time to mend."

"I don't know if I'll ever completely trust Tracy again," Amy verifies. "I go on living day to day, wondering about tomorrow."

"It puts us in a terrible bind," says Tracy's father, Henry, who has obviously made greater strides in coming to terms with the past. "She bought a house, and I cosigned. I thought there'd be no problem. The very day we bought the house, she was under the influence of drugs, and I didn't know it. She tried to protect me. I don't have much money. But the foreclosure drained a lot from us. We also paid the attorney's fees. She's trying to pay us back now."

"When you're an addict," Tracy reflects, "you think, 'Well, if I want to hurt myself, that's my own business.' You don't really realize how devastating your behavior is to everyone around you."

"Of course we wondered where we had failed in her upbringing," Henry continues, "but it wasn't like that. We're Christian people, and she was raised in the church. We, at least *I*, don't feel we did anything wrong. And I think we went about the fifth mile. She'd tell you the same thing. It broke our hearts. When you love someone who just ruins their life, it's a little hard to take."

"It's ruined *my* life. I will never be the same, and I will never get over it," insists Amy. "I'm bitter. My marriage is ruined, and all my dreams are shattered. How could such a thing happen to such a lovely girl with so many advantages in life?

"I feel I was a wonderful mother, and anyone who knows me says I'm a good mother," she emphasizes. "But even if it happens again, we're going to be right in there because that's a mother and father's love. I don't know how anyone could do otherwise.

"And I don't know what she would have done without us because all her friends left her. I'm just thankful my mother died before all this happened. She loved Tracy so much; she was the favorite of all her grandchildren."

While living with her parents, Tracy went back to school and became a paralegal. But soon enough she began longing to go back to nursing. Her license had been suspended for a mandatory three years, but the law specifies that during the last year, a person can enter treatment and—with clean urines for that entire year—apply for reinstatement of license.

Tracy was required to pay for her own therapy and psychological evaluation, which was to be submitted to the state board of nursing for its evaluation. She was also required to take continuing-education classes to enable her to re-enter nursing.

After a five-year probation period she is now required to give urine samples regularly, without any advance notice, and to continue her therapy. Her nursing supervisor is required to file a quarterly report on her job performance with the state nursing board. But today both her professional and personal lives have stabilized.

"I'm in a stable, caring relationship with a woman who doesn't use. We've been together for five years. I love being a nurse, and I have a different attitude today," maintains Tracy, who, though sober since 1983, still admits to craving cocaine.

"I'm finally growing up and becoming an adult, and I feel really good about myself now. But I guess it's the old cliché, 'You learn from bad experiences.'"

And there is no doubt that Tracy learned the hard way. In fact, in periods when she feels particularly susceptible to her addiction, she uses Antabuse as further assurance she won't be tempted to use. Antabuse, a drug that reacts to even the slightest amount of alcohol, makes a person violently ill.

"Just to cover myself, I go on Antabuse over the holidays, starting in November. I haven't done drugs or cocaine in years. But there are times when I wake up and I think of doing cocaine. It's amazing to me that I still react that way.

"But looking at my veins sometimes when it's hot and they stick out, it's like I have a physiological rush. And it stems from cocaine, not Demerol or anything else. It almost ruined me. It's a very dangerous drug."

DIANA

FINANCIAL LOAN ANALYST
LOS ANGELES, CALIFORNIA

Diana, now 27, was 22 years old and had been using for 10 years when she finally admitted she was addicted to cocaine and alcohol and went to Alcoholics Anonymous for help. Her childhood had been rather avant-garde, but not extreme. She and her sister, who also used but never became addicted, grew up in a loving, upper-middle-class home, not on the streets. Unbeknownst to the family for many years, however, her father was also a cocaine addict and had used heavily for more than two decades. Her parents divorced when Diana was 13, but during her late teens she and her father used together. Her mother, unable to stop her and unaware of her father's contribution to the problem, watched helplessly. Addiction, the entire family agrees, tore them all apart. Today they share sobriety and a newfound relationship. This is the story as told by each member of the family.

Diana first started popping pills when she was just 12 years old. Most of the pills came from the medicine cabinets of her friends' parents. Some of the drugs she and her friends bought on the street.

When she bottomed out early, at age 22, Diana was addicted primarily to cocaine and alcohol. Everyone could see long before that she was going down fast—everyone except Diana and her father, also a cocaine addict and alcoholic.

111

"When it really took off was in junior high," recalls Diana, who works today as an accountant for an exclusive furniture manufacturer based in Beverly Hills. "It wasn't very typical for me growing up at all. I never went to class, I didn't participate in school activities, I just hung out with the drug addicts outside.

"It wasn't so hard to get drugs then. There wasn't this war on drugs like there is now. Pills were most prevalent because people's mothers and fathers were taking them left and right. I mean Valium, Quaaludes, Percodan, and Tuinal—you could get them out of the medicine cabinet, and that's what we did. And alcohol was very readily available."

Diana's mother, Rita, who works as office manager for an L.A.-based plastic surgeon, doesn't do drugs and drinks very little. Although she knew her husband smoked marijuana, she didn't know for many years that he "was into heavy drugs like cocaine." They had been divorced for two or three years when she realized the extent of his addiction.

For several years Rita was also completely unaware of her daughter's drug and alcohol use, and she still has no idea where Diana got the pills. "There could have been Valium in the house," says Rita thoughtfully. "The only time I ever took Valium was when I got on an airplane. But I absolutely was not taking on a regular basis. Certainly, after I knew she was into drugs, I wouldn't have kept it in a place she could get to it. But at 13 years old, I honestly did not know."

"In those days," chimes in her father, Harry, a 46-year-old international marketing specialist, "most housewives had drugs in the house, but they didn't even know they *were* drugs."

Eventually, Rita could no longer deny her daughter had a serious problem. "I remember confronting her about drinking because I was very concerned about her driving. I took her car away a number of times. But I knew she had a drug problem, a serious drug problem, when she started threatening to commit suicide. I think she was 15 at the time.

"Even then I didn't know it was as serious as it was, even though her grades were bad—all the telltale signs. Maybe it was just the old story: I didn't want to face it. So I said, 'No, it can't be. I mean, she gets up in the morning and she comes home at night. She seems to function pretty well.' After she recovered and I first heard how heavily she used, I was shocked. Absolutely shocked."

"Nobody wants to believe that your perfect little child is doing drugs," Diana says, recounting how easily she hid her behavior in the beginning. She credits her open-structure private school with not only making it child's play to hide her drug abuse, but also with providing opportunity for it to flourish.

"It was very progressive. You moved at your own pace, called teachers by their first names, went to class outside. I was also in classes with kids much older, and that had a lot to do with where I got drugs. They introduced me to pot, alcohol, and stuff like that. I sought out people like me who drank and partied."

Not only was Diana's school structure rather permissive, her home life was also rather loose. Her father traveled extensively for his job and wasn't around much to discipline her or her younger sister, Tina. Her parents separated when she was 10 years old, after which time Harry began making huge amounts of money and was extremely generous with his family. This cash made drugs even more accessible. As her mother slowly became aware of Diana's drug and alcohol abuse and came out of her own denial, she found her daughter completely unmanageable.

"I knew she was probably trying grass," Rita admits, "but to be honest, I thought alcohol was more of a problem. You really can't tell someone is stoned unless you look in their eyes. I mean they don't fall down, slur their words, and vomit. But with alcohol they do. Many times Diana would come home and literally be barely able to make her way upstairs. Then she'd immediately go into the bathroom and start throwing up. She was running wild. I caught her hitching, which scared me more than *anything*, but I had *no* idea that she was into cocaine.

"For years I took her to psychologists, I talked to her, I punished her, I bribed her. I did everything I could possibly do to get her to straighten out. You name it, there was nothing I didn't say to her and nothing I didn't offer her. But none of it worked."

Diana recalls the first time her mother confronted her, around age 16, and her vehement denial that she had any kind of problem. She was standing in the bathroom of her family's home, staring intently into the mirror, noting how bad she looked.

"It was the first time I saw a noticeable change in my appearance. My mother came up behind me, and I'll never forget this. She looked into my eyes in the mirror, and she said, 'I think you're an alcoholic.' I screamed, 'You don't know what you're talking about! You're out of your mind! You're crazy! Leave me alone!' But something registered."

Diana was introduced to cocaine by a high school boyfriend who had extremely wealthy parents from whom he stole money to buy drugs. While she can't bring to mind her very first experience with cocaine, she does think of those days as a period of tremendous upheaval.

"I was a garbage-can addict," she says. "I took everything and anything. It just didn't matter to me. Even if I didn't like it, I'd take it. I don't remember the *very* first time, but cocaine slowly became very pleasant, almost euphoric. I just loved it, and of course I craved it more and more. It's very addictive.

"There was also a ritual and a lot of stigma attached to it. Now it's a very low-class drug, with freebasing and rock cocaine, but it wasn't like that in the late seventies. It was very exclusive, and it was a big deal. Rock stars and movie stars did it. It made us feel very important. I loved it. I just *loved* it!"

Diana's entire family feels that her father's addiction sanctified drug use in the minds of Diana and her sister. While his usage wasn't "out in the open until their late teens," they were somehow aware of it, everyone agrees, and eventually, unbeknownst to their mother, the two girls began using drugs—first pot and later cocaine—in the presence of their father. While he didn't introduce them to these substances, he did supply the drugs on these occasions.

Her father used cocaine for more than 20 years, beginning in the mid-to-late sixties, a time when cocaine was almost unheard-of. "I started doing cocaine before it was in vogue," Harry recalls. "You didn't find many people around who had it or even knew what it was. It was cheap. It wasn't in demand. I used to pay $800 an ounce. I couldn't even go into the bathroom in a club or public place without half the people there following me in. My friend and I were probably the biggest coke users in Beverly Hills at one time. We've probably turned more people on to coke than a dealer."

Harry quit doing coke only a year and a half ago, shocked by the death of his business partner who suffered a stroke in his mid-40's, induced by cocaine use. It was after his divorce from Diana's mother in 1974 that his own habit escalated. At that time he was making a great deal of money, very quickly, in real estate, most of which went to support his ever-growing drug habit. A few years later Diana discovered her father's cocaine use while visiting his home.

"I think I found a vial of cocaine while I was looking for a joint or pills, maybe Valium. Plus, there are some very telltale signs. His nose was always running, or he was sniffing; he drank most of the dinners my family went to with him, smoked a lot. Being on cocaine myself, I was able to recognize them.

"It was all very, very cool to me," Diana says almost fondly. "He was in a very high-pressure job, made a lot of money very quickly, and he hung out with a lot of very famous people. It was this very glamorous thing. Because he had a lot of money, he had very clean cocaine. It was very good, and we *loved* to do my dad's cocaine."

Her sister, Tina, now 23, got involved with drugs at an equally early age. She credits both a "nonaddictive personality" and luck for never becoming an abuser herself. In her late teens she simply lost interest in using drugs and drinking. But she recalls vividly, "We used to have an attitude that we had a cool dad who parties, and so maybe I'll be cool if I do it too."

Tina never spoke to her mother about Diana's obviously increasing problem because "she and I were good about that. We didn't tell on each other. But when I was very young, it scared the hell out of me! I was just so freaked out and shocked by the whole thing. Later I really got into it, and I used to party with Diana. But I got lucky, I went through my stage and walked away from it."

"No question about it," affirms mother Rita, who blames her ex-husband's drug abuse for many things, but not for the breakup of their marriage. "Diana's father lived in the fast lane, doing things you read about in books—private jets, big money, affluent people, and drugs everywhere. Most of his money went up his nose, but he lived and functioned, made money, and took care of us from afar. Diana saw that and figured she would be okay too. I think that had a lot to do with it."

Rita knew that all her family members smoked marijuana, at least on an occasional basis. But she *was* entirely unaware that her husband was using cocaine with her children, and she was "fit to be tied" when she found out. "I trusted him that he had some sort of sanity to know this was not something he did with his daughters. He said, 'Look, she's going to do it anyway; so better she do it with me. At least I know what I'm giving her is clean stuff. It's not going to kill her, and she's not getting it from her punk friends off the street.' I absolutely did not approve, but there was nothing I could do. I was always the bad guy, the villain. It was very difficult for me to watch."

Today Tina empathizes with her mother's plight in earlier years. "My mother didn't know that my father used to do drugs with us. She knew that we used to smoke pot together because we did it in front of her. She didn't approve of it, but it was just accepted. She *didn't* know we did cocaine."

Their father doesn't really remember too much about his family's discovery of his drug use. Extended cocaine and alcohol abuse have impaired his memory of that time frame. Now living in Las Vegas, Nevada, he's hazy on many points.

"My memory is really distorted," says Harry, who claims he did from one to two ounces of cocaine a week. "I was making almost half a million dollars a year and spending close to that on coke.

"You think nobody knows, except everybody does. I think the kids saw my habit. Maybe not directly, because I was trying to hide it, but they were quite aware that I was doing something. I think it's the old story, 'If it's okay for Dad, it's okay for me. Why can't I do it if he does it? He has so much fun with it.'

"Eventually, I probably started doing cocaine in front of them because I was sick and tired of stepping out of the room every 10 minutes. So the hell with it. It's not that I didn't care, it was just past the point. They weren't dumb. They didn't think I had a cold for 10 years. They knew something was wrong. I would sneak, and they would catch me.

"And it was just such a part of my life," he says matter-of-factly. "I just never left home without it. It got to the point where I would do it in a public restaurant or anyplace. That's how hip, slick, and cool I thought I was."

Diana, Tina, and Harry all mention the Christmas when he gave them and their friends about half an ounce of cocaine as a gift. He just walked into their apartment and dumped it on the coffee table and said, "Merry Christmas."

Diana's response: "I thought, 'Oh, my God, I've got the best dad in the world! Look what he just did for us, you guys. He loves me so much.' That's how distorted it had become. I was so proud that my friends were there to see it. But it was so disgusting. That's a sick thing to do with your father."

Tina and her father look back on the evening in an entirely different light. For Harry, "it was just like the end of everything."

Tina felt her father's distress that night. "He was going through this whole dilemma. He wouldn't even do it with us. It was very uncomfortable for him."

"I know that now, because we've talked about that evening," Diana adds sadly, "and it was very significant for both of us. He knew inherently it was wrong. He felt awful, remorseful, dirty, and that he had failed as a parent."

According to Rita, her ex-husband helped assuage his guilt by being exceptionally generous with his family financially. This also helped Diana support her habit, as did the fact that her father kept as much as a kilo of coke around and never noticed if some of the supply was missing.

Eventually, Diana developed a 2½-to-3-gram-a-day habit. By then she was stealing cocaine from her father, and the two of them were using together regularly from his supply.

"I had a lot of guilt," Harry admits. "I guess in my own crazy way I was showing off. In my opinion if I try to tell another father/daughter or father/son that they're ruining their child's life, getting them into coke, I don't think they would see it. I think they would be as blind as I was.

"That's how powerful and crazy the whole thing is. I was in such denial, there was no way I could admit she was hooked. I remember one time she told me she thought she had a problem, and I said, 'You can't have a problem, you only spend a few hundred dollars a week. I spend thousands a week. How can you have a problem if I don't?' In my mind, to this day, I can't believe that she was hooked on coke. That's how crazy it is."

Today Diana recognizes her former drug abuse as the most effective way she could get her father's attention. "It was the only way I thought I could have a relationship with him. That was how I got love and attention, by drinking and using with him. That was the only level I could relate to him on. I was a drug addict and an alcoholic, he was a drug addict and an alcoholic, and we had something in common."

Her father feels that he was able to overlook even the most obvious parental duties for two reasons: cocaine had distorted his reason, and addicts become totally self-focused. An addict's only concern is for him- or herself and the next fix. Additionally, Harry was dating girls younger than Diana and hardly considered her a dependent.

"Cocaine was just part of the party. I wasn't a very nice person. To be very honest, I was turning on young girls with coke, and I didn't care if they were 16, 17, or 18. It was the greatest way in the world to get a girl into bed. I probably went through as many women as I did coke."

As Diana grew older, graduated from high school, and embarked on a career, her addictive relationship with her father took on new dimensions. She "credits" her father with teaching her how to survive her habit and chosen lifestyle, although it was apparently something he did unconsciously.

"He taught me how to live that kind of life, how to be around those kinds of people, how to avoid traps I would have fallen into, how to stay ahead of the game, how to survive. And for a drug addict/alcoholic, that's really a basic instinct. It's what we know best. In a lot of ways I think he saved my life—many times.

"He just taught me things I wouldn't have known. Like he once said to me, 'If you're going to try heroin, come to me. Don't go buy it from somebody on the street, because you'll get stuff that was made in some bathtub. I can get you pure heroin.'

"Obviously, some things I had to go through for myself. It was all part of this degradation, my self-destruct, and he couldn't have told me, 'Don't do that.' I would use his name to get into the clubs on Sunset Boulevard, and I'd get into real binds. I'd end up going home with men for cocaine and freebase and got beat up a lot.

"He would also take me to places where there were girls like me, my age, who were walking around like zombies, with no clothes and little bikinis. All these young girls were with middle-aged men who probably had daughters their age. He took me there to show me how *not* to become. It was his way of saying, 'Grow up and marry a nice Jewish boy.'

"But they were prostitutes, and *that* was the difference," she emphasizes. "Although I did anything I had to—and I did sleep with a lot of people just to get cocaine and to stay loaded—it wasn't my job. I was in a legitimate profession."

At the time Diana was working in a high-level position as a loan analyst for a large national corporation based in L.A. In her daily work she was responsible for the handling of millions and millions of dollars. She was in constant contact with extremely wealthy and influential clients. Eventually, her addiction affected her ability to function at work.

"Once I got addicted, I absolutely needed it to survive. I thought it made it easier to go to work, to talk to clients, to get through the day. I began to use heavily on a daily basis. I was doing it at lunch. Forget lunch—there were times that I would be up all night freebasing, and I'd literally take a hit from the pipe, hold it in, and run out of the house into my car to go to work. In my car, I'd hold my breath with that hit, ready to pass out.

"Then I'd have a quarter or half gram in my pocket or my briefcase to sustain me through the day. I was always in the bathroom, but I'd go one floor below or one floor up and two floors below. I'd get through that and have the dealer deliver to work. Or I would take my boss's car and go get more. I'd leave at lunch and drink just to take the edge off. I would take two- or three-hour lunches and go to my dealer's house and just snort my brains out.

"There were days that I couldn't even make it to work. Sometimes I couldn't talk to clients on the phone because my voice was shaking so badly. Sometimes I couldn't even hold the phone. I couldn't write. I would try to do things that didn't require speech, coordination, or concentration, which was just about everything. I could still think, but I had a really hard time with my motor functions.

"Plus my temper. I was so short-tempered from the cocaine and drinking and lack of sleep that I had trouble dealing with clients. I got frustrated very easily. And I dealt with a lot of cash and some very important clients.

"I can't explain what it's like," Diana pauses, searching for the right words. "When you're on cocaine, it's not like being drunk or on a lot of Valium. You're very coherent, and it's frustrating because there's something going on inside of you that's screaming, absolutely screaming, but you can't communicate. I made a lot of serious mistakes."

Diana once came to the office on a Saturday to make up for time lost while she was out "sick" and ended up doing coke at her desk, "where anybody could walk in," because she didn't have time to go to the bathroom. Her addiction was so complete that she linked her drug abuse in her mind with her professional success. "It's funny," she says ironically, "I thought I had really 'arrived' when I was on my lunch hour one day and went to a paraphernalia store. I bought some of those little vials with the coke spoons attached and put them in my briefcase. In my briefcase were all these very important papers and appointment books and also my cocaine. It was in its place like everything else, like a Cross pen. I was in a business suit, in my car, going to meetings and sniffing while I was driving. I thought that's what being an executive was all about.

"At corporate Christmas dinners I would get drunk at the party, be in the bathroom all night doing cocaine, and leave with some industry executive to sleep with him. But first we'd stop at the dealer's, and I'd make sure he bought me cocaine before I would sleep with him."

While Diana marvels that she didn't lose her job, she explains that she intentionally ingratiated herself with her employers to avoid being fired. Her manager, she relates, thought of her as a daughter.

"I was functioning. I never thought about not working. It was important not to lose my job, because if I did, it meant that I had a problem. I was covering up, and my manager also covered for me. She saved my ass many, many times. I always told people that I had allergies, because my nose was so out of control. They all knew that I had a problem, but I was still functioning, and I was good at what I did.

"Also," she states with no pride whatsoever, "being the conniving and manipulative drug addict that I was, I was able to crawl under their skins. I made them sort of love me so they wouldn't fire me."

Diana realizes now that if they had fired her, she would have probably hit her bottom much more quickly and gone for help much earlier. She was addicted for 10 years by the time she sought help at Cocaine Anonymous, Alcoholics Anonymous, and, years later, Adult Children of Alcoholics.

Diana, who also gave up a two-pack-a-day smoking habit two years ago, began to suffer from severe health problems related to drug and alcohol abuse around this time, and her finances were in ruins. "I was forever broke because all my money went up my nose," she laments. "I wasn't eating or sleeping regularly. I was irritable, had migraine headaches, stomach problems, bleeding gums, and I shook constantly. I vomited *all* the time, and it was not self-induced. I probably threw up every night, and it was always after several hours of drinking and doing cocaine. I would just start to gag and vomit. Then I'd feel much better and just keep going, doing more cocaine and drinking.

"I lied all the time and would forget whom I had lied to about what. At the end it became very sad because in a moment of clarity I saw me from the outside, and I had become everything I hated. I was a liar, a thief, and an absolute slave to the freebase pipe and coke."

At the height of her addiction Diana's family and friends were all trying to help her. She lost many friends along the way. In the end cocaine was no longer a social event for her. She suffered in her addiction entirely alone.

"I had a lot of friends who had known me all my life and who wouldn't be with me anymore because every time we went out, I had to have cocaine. It was okay with alcohol because even if I drank the whole bottle, they would have a drink or two. But I had to have cocaine all the time. It became a drag to be with me. I just realized I couldn't be around people anymore. I was doing a lot of cocaine, but I was by myself doing it."

Diana began suffering extreme depressions, often calling one of her few remaining friends in the middle of the night, crying hysterically. Finally, a grammar school friend who had moved away many years ago returned to Los Angeles and convinced Diana that she needed help.

"She came back into my life, and she saw that I was absolutely a disaster. One night she called and said 'I'm going to come over and pick you up at 7:30. You have a problem, and I think you need to go to a 12-Step meeting.'

"I remember coming home from work and making a drink. She took me to a meeting, and that was it. It was a Tuesday night, January 1984, and that was the last drink I ever had. I remember, after my first meeting I told my mom it was the first time I had been straight for two or three days in a row since I was 12 years old. She just cried."

Just as Diana credited her father with helping her survive her addiction, she credits her mother with helping her survive her sobriety. The emotional support was crucial.

"My mother saw a really beautiful person inside of me that I couldn't see or get in touch with. She believed I could make it, even when I didn't believe it. She unconditionally loved me, and her strength kept me going."

Her mother points out that an addiction in the family destroys the entire family. "It's not just the person using the drugs, it's everyone around her. It's so much conflict and so much pain and anger. A marriage is constant work anyway, even without this horrible, horrible thing happening right before your eyes. It's a 24-hour disease that never stops.

"From that first meeting Diana never took a drink, a pill, or a snort of coke. Nothing! To this day I'm absolutely amazed that she was able to do it—I can't even tell you. But I thank God every day. She turned out to be the most fantastic human being, and I am so proud of her."

Although sober since early 1984, Diana is quick to point out that it's been an uphill and ongoing battle. Her newfound sobriety estranged her from her father for several years until he also became sober. Although they are extremely close today, it was a tremendous strain on their relationship at the time.

Her sobriety was further tested when two nonelective surgeries made it necessary for her to take the painkiller Demerol, which she immediately gave to a roommate, who doled out the prescribed dosage at the prescribed hours. Her medication was also cut off long before it would have been for other, nonaddicted patients.

To further distance herself from her addiction, Diana changed her job, her place of residence, and her friends. It was a time of great upheaval, and even today she battles temptation on a day-to-day basis.

"I could not have done it without the 12-Step program, and I couldn't stay sober today on my own. It's not as if I'm dependent on it, like it's this cult thing. But it is the crux of my sobriety.

"I'm learning coping skills there. So although the things that I go through in life may seem disastrous in sobriety, I can deal with them anyway. I have this faith that everything is going to be okay. It may not turn out how I want it, but it's going to turn out okay."

When Diana describes the strained relations with her father back then, she first mentions that they spoke only yesterday. She called him to exalt over another milestone in her sobriety, an event of little note, she admits, to someone not "working the program."

"It wasn't literally that he wouldn't talk to me, but our conversations were very curt. And I couldn't be around him, because he was always loaded. It was getting worse, and I hated seeing him like that. We had a relationship, but it was really a drag. He didn't want to hear about my sobriety."

Harry is uncomfortable talking about this extremely awkward time and prefers to talk about their relationship today. "We've never been so close. I guess, when I think back on it, I just saw myself in her, and I didn't want to face it."

He also admits that although she was his daughter, he felt a macho negativity toward her drug use even while excusing his own behavior, a commonly held attitude among male addicts.

"I was cool, but I thought women who used drugs were slobs. And I thought Diana was a total slob by being drunk too. See, in my mind I was together, but she was not. I think that's just straight macho. I can drink and smoke, but a woman shouldn't."

"You know, it's not perfect," Diana contributes. "There's a lot of work because there's been a lot of damage from what we went through together. But there's a bond between us that's very special because we share this disease and we share sobriety. There are things that just he and I know about because of the disease. Despair, hopelessness, and self-hate you can't know unless you've been at the bottom. And the courage it takes to stay sober a day at a time. We talk about it a lot, about sobriety, and it's really very special."

In fact, Diana's outlook on her entire way of life has changed dramatically. No longer looking to live in the fast lane, she now leads a much less hectic and healthier lifestyle.

"My priorities have changed a lot. It's more quiet for me now. I just want to settle down. Most important, at night I go to bed with peace in my head and soul. I wake up most of the time happy and ready for the day. I'm not in fear, and I don't wake up depressed. I will always have this disease, but it's like a remission. I get a daily reprieve."

KIM

COLLEGE STUDENT AND WAITRESS
NASHVILLE, TENNESSEE

Kim, now 26, grew up in one of Nashville's best suburban neighborhoods, the product of a respectable middle-class upbringing. She was 15 when she first rebelled against her overprotective parents and began using marijuana. By 18 she was not only taking hard drugs, but was also dealing them. As her addiction worsened, she even participated in a drugstore robbery. By the age of 20 she had dropped out of the top-ranked college she attended and was deeply addicted to both intravenous cocaine use, approximately three grams a day, and narcotics. Her parents denied that she had a problem and never intervened. Eventually, she was arrested for forging prescriptions. Her week-long incarceration, where she suffered an incapacitating withdrawal and sexual harassment from her jailers, shocked her sober. Today, clean since 1983, she is a registered nurse in a Nashville-based Care Unit, helping other addicts.

"It wasn't until I had some clean time behind me that I said, 'Whoa. What happened? How did I end up there?' " drawls Kim in a long, slow southern accent. She was one of two children born to a high school guidance counselor's secretary and a retail salesman, who both thought smoking cigarettes was a moral transgression.

"I had sort of accepted drug addiction as my fate, but at the same time, with my background, I felt I wasn't like other addicts. I mean, I'm like them in that I'm an addict, but I had a lot better things socially than most of them did. You couldn't say, 'She's from a bad family; so that's why she came out that way.' "

Kim had been introduced to marijuana at age 16 by a cousin, and she liked what it did to her. She knew that her brother, six years older and attending the prestigious Vanderbilt University in the family's hometown of Nashville, smoked pot, and that somehow sanctified it. Within months Kim was doing "whatever was on the street," including Quaaludes, Valium, and LSD. She smoked marijuana on a daily basis.

"I got the money from my parents by telling them I was going out to do something. Sometimes I stole money out of my mother's purse. I think she had to notice, but she never said anything. My parents have always been the type of people who blamed my friends for whatever trouble I got into. Their solution was not to punish me. It's curious. I think they saw changes in me but didn't want to look at them. They had to know.

"My mom didn't want me to grow up. She wanted to protect me from the world and keep me from getting hurt or into trouble. I was never brought up to make my own decisions or even to make my own bed. My way to handle it was to do drugs. I had control in the drug world. I had power among my friends. I had a whole other life that my parents didn't know about."

Kim's mother was so manipulative that, without permission, she sent an application and her daughter's high school records to Vanderbilt. She even went so far as to hide correspondence to her daughter from the out-of-state schools to which Kim had applied. Drug abuse had not affected Kim's top-notch grades, and she won a full-tuition scholarship to the selective Vanderbilt, the same school Kim's mother had earlier railroaded her older brother into attending.

"Everybody seemed to know what I wanted to do, and here I was, at the top of my class, and I had no idea," she bemoans. "Deep down, what I wanted to do was take some time off and just figure out what I wanted to do.

"The crucial thing for my mom was not my going to Vanderbilt because of its prestige. She just wanted me here in Nashville. At that point what I needed was to grow independent of my parents. But I didn't have a choice; so I thought Vanderbilt was my only way out of the house. I was grasping for control. It went back and forth, back and forth. I guess the ultimate revenge for her making me go to Vanderbilt was that I screwed it up real bad."

Kim's drug use escalated as soon as she took up residence in a campus dorm. Although her roommates were "real straight, they didn't even drink," no one ever confronted Kim about her self-destructive behavior.

"Vanderbilt is very upper-middle-class, very conservative, very Republican, and I felt inadequate. My feelings of inferiority went sky high. But on the flip side, I felt very superior streetwise. There were people around me who had never taken a drink.

"I went there one semester, and I don't think I finished any of my classes. About mid-semester I even quit going. I slept during the day. I knew something bad was going to happen, but I just did not look ahead, period. I didn't care what my parents thought. I didn't care about bringing home Fs."

Kim found two friends with whom she could share her drug abuse. One was an alcoholic from a small town in Tennessee. She and Kim met nightly at the college pub, where they drank and smoked pot. The second girl, from Miami, introduced Kim to cocaine.

"I had just never had the exposure to cocaine during my teenage years, but I knew back then that my brother was doing cocaine, and that's something I had always wondered about. It seemed mysterious, something so small and so expensive. And here was my brother, who was in college at Vanderbilt and whom everybody was so proud of, doing it. So it sort of reinforced it with me that it was okay. I don't really know if he went over the edge or not. He smokes a little pot occasionally. He drinks a lot."

Although already heavily into the use of narcotics, the attendant addiction to cocaine proved her downfall. She was 20 years old, and it was the final year of her using.

"I had seen coke before and tried sniffing it over the years, but it never really did anything for me. Then I met this girl from Miami, and we got to be good friends. We lived on the same floor in the dorm. At the time she was somebody who seemed to have it together. She wasn't addicted, she did her work, and it didn't seem to affect her life. She just used it for fun on the weekends, a sort of status symbol thing."

But for Kim it was an instantaneous addiction that advanced her erratic behavior to disastrous proportions. "I remember snorting it and getting high and thinking, 'Oh, this is what they're talking about.' I think, with her being from Miami, it was the first good coke that I had ever had, and it was really fun. I had a really good time. The other stuff I had in high school had been cut by punks selling drugs.

"After a certain point, and I don't know when I crossed that point, I made the commitment to just do drugs. That was my life's focus. After a while, when any emotions crept up, such as pain or remorse, I just did drugs."

At one point Kim, who considered herself the average, American girl next door, acted as the driver in a drugstore robbery. A male counterpart and a female friend of his who worked in the pharmacy actually broke in after hours and took the pills. They were never caught. Although Kim had been able to push her values aside far enough to participate in the felonious act, the guilt afterward overwhelmed her.

"I just flipped out. I realized what a deep mess I had gotten into. I had some sense of clarity that what was happening wasn't right. It was near the end of the semester, nothing important, just finals week," she laughs, "and I packed and went home to my parents' house."

Kim spent three months completely bedridden by depression. She was so down that she didn't even bother to do drugs. Day in and day out she stared at a television set. Still her parents did nothing to intervene.

"I went home, and I wouldn't talk about it. Of course I couldn't go to my parents, who freaked if I smoked a cigarette, and say, 'Look, I just helped rob a drugstore.' For three months I hardly got out of bed. I just couldn't function. I watched TV all day and all night long.

"I remember something coming on the public-TV channel about depression. This checklist—you know, if you've got over five of these symptoms, you're clinically depressed and need help from a psychiatrist. Well, I had all of them. I needed help then. I needed my parents to intervene, but they didn't."

After three months Kim pulled herself together enough to get a job and move out of her parents' house. She began waitressing at a newly opened Mexican restaurant.

"Job orientation was my first real contact with people for months. It really felt good, and I began to have a sense that I was going to be okay. And when I saw the money start to roll in from this job, I saw my way out of my parents' house."

Without a rental history or car Kim's housing choices were limited, and she ended up in a dingy, one-room apartment across the street from her job. Her parents were angry with her for moving out, and she felt overwhelmingly alone.

"It was a really long, cold, depressing winter. At least I remember it that way," she laments. "I just felt awfully alone. I started my drug use really heavy—cocaine and Dilaudid daily."

Dilaudid is a narcotic that provides an intense high for the first four hours and "good feelings" for the next four hours. Kim was doing four milligrams of Dilaudid twice a day to enhance her continuous use of cocaine, which eventually peaked at three grams per day.

"It was the best high," Kim says fondly. "Cocaine combined with Dilaudid gives you a nice, sleepy kind of long-term feeling. The high from coke is gone in 15 or 20 minutes, and you want more right away. And it's a really uncomfortable thing to come down from. You get nervous and have the jitters, and you're grinding your jaw. You just feel real uncomfortable, and you want more real bad. If you use coke on top of Dilaudid, when you're coming down, it's not that bad. You have something that kicks in to soften the blow."

Though Kim's drug addiction was continuing to escalate rapidly, she also continued to perform well at work. The coke made her more gregarious; so she sold food well and made above-average money.

"I would do a lot of coke at work and make a lot more tips. I could talk to people and con them. When I met someone, I would start figuring out ways I could get over on them if they had anything to offer me. And the money helped support my habit."

Eventually, she stole $60 and a codeine prescription from a co-worker's purse left in the woman's locker. While she was never directly accused, her employers and co-workers knew she was responsible. Still, Kim felt no guilt for her actions.

"I thought, 'Well, she shouldn't have left her purse in the locker,'" she shrugs. "You can always talk yourself out of it." Kim began dealing drugs again to support her habit and fell in with a group of musicians who were injecting cocaine. One of them later became her live-in boyfriend.

"My boyfriend was one of the group that used I.V. Seeing what they felt made me want to do it. It was like, 'Gasp, oh, my God!' Doing cocaine that way made it a whole different feeling. It was a whole lot better than snorting it. I never freebased, 'cause it wasn't around back then. But people talk about the pipe today as if it's the same sort of addiction as the needle. It's the same sort of immediate rush.

"I had gotten into something a little over my head, but on the flip side, there's something about doing drugs, being a subculture. It's like a secret club that nobody else knows about. I felt that these people were at the center of this secret club. They were using drugs the most direct way you could use them and getting the most benefit from them. I was getting my money's worth, and I wasn't wasting any."

After her boyfriend moved in, their addictive personalities fed off their mutual drug abuse. "We dealt drugs together—pot, Dilaudid, and a little cocaine. But I'd always end up doing the coke before I sold it. I really felt a love for him, as much as I could feel at the time. It was more than just a convenient situation, but I don't know what the quality of my love was."

Apparently, there was quality to their love. Subsequently they were arrested together, became sober together, and in 1984 they married. But before going straight, their addictions would plummet them even further into despair.

"At first I didn't really think about it," Kim shivers, "but towards the end I realized it was starting to get weird. People I was around were carrying guns and becoming intensely paranoid. The people I had started out having some sort of bond or trust with were now the people I didn't trust at all.

"But on the other hand, I understood them. I could not leave my house, go to the store, and leave one of them there with my cocaine, or they would do it all. But on the flip side, I understood that when you're doing drugs, there aren't any rules. I couldn't blame them, because if I had been at their house, I would have done the same thing. But the people kept getting stranger and stranger. Before our eyes, we saw them transform into these really paranoid, dangerous people."

One of the people who most frightened Kim came to the apartment one day in an attempt to sell them a .357 Magnum pistol. They turned him down. The very next evening he went to the home of a nightclub owner, whom he shot and killed in order to steal a large cache of cocaine and the man's gold jewelry.

"Right before this he had also broken into our apartment and stolen our pistol and about four pounds of pot we had. We were deep in the hole because we owed for this pot. We made the decision together that we had to get out of this.

"My boyfriend had been down the road of cocaine and Dilaudid addiction before, and he knew more than I did that there was no end to it. Or if it did end, it wouldn't be good. But at the time there weren't any Care Unit commercials on TV. It wasn't cool to be clean."

Together, they signed on at a methadone clinic; however, the counseling consisted of "a group of addicts, sitting around talking about using," which made Kim want to use even more. They remained straight, with the exception of drinking a lot of beer, for only a week. Soon after, Kim and her boyfriend began forging prescriptions for narcotics.

"I took one prescription I had gotten from a doctor. I whited-out his writing, and I took it to the library and made a copy of it. Then I cut it out real carefully and took a red crayon and made a mark on the top of it, as if it had been torn off a pad, and it worked."

Kim recalls a college psychology professor who found the manipulative behavior of addicts exceptionally innovative and resourceful. "He really believed that addicts were smarter than everybody else because they had been forced to think more to get drugs. He thought that if all the addicts cleaned up, they could be the great leaders of the world."

The long arm of the law did catch up with them, however, and Kim was arrested for forgery. But she spent only a few hours in jail before she was rescued by her parents. Again, they did not confront their daughter about her behavior. "They bailed me out of jail, I yelled at them, and they left," she recalls incredulously.

A month and a half later, Kim, along with her boyfriend this time, was again arrested for forging prescriptions. For a second offense she was facing a lengthy incarceration. At her request her parents enlisted the aid of a lawyer who had represented a friend of Kim's. In the meantime, she spent a week in a rural jailhouse. She classifies her ensuing withdrawal, along with her debilitating depression some months earlier, as the worst experiences in her life.

"I guess my main priority was getting along with the other girls in jail. At first I was scared of them, but I think they were more scared of me, which kind of amused me. I was like a big-time criminal or something. It was a small, countrylike jail, and most of them were in for things like stealing from K-Mart.

"There was one girl who was retarded or something. You could tell she was really slow. She followed me around, and it really got on my nerves because I was withdrawing. She asked me what I was in for, and I turned to her and told her I had killed five people," Kim laughs nervously. "I didn't have any more trouble out of her. She just went away.

"There wasn't any detox. Death didn't enter my mind. But looking back, it scares me because that could have happened. I could have had a seizure. My bones hurt. I felt like I was hurting from the inside. I know now that was muscle aches. I couldn't eat or sleep. It got to the point where I was dreaming while I was awake. It was like doing hallucinogenics. I didn't see my jailmates turn into anything. It was nothing scary, just dots, flashes, and colors that I knew weren't there.

"Dilaudid addiction messes up all the fluids in your body. So when you come off it, everything that is fluid balanced, which is everything, is out of kilter. So the main thing I got was the sweats. I'd get cold and shiver. I couldn't ever get warm. And my stomach was in a knot the whole week. Today, when patients in treatment piss and moan about getting some Tylenol for their headache, I have to bite my tongue."

In addition to how uncomfortable Kim was physically, she was also emotionally strained, not knowing what to expect from the future. "The withdrawal was coupled with the fact that the whole week, I knew my life was going to take a drastic change, and I had no idea that things were going to be okay. I didn't have a whole lot of vision about getting my life together. I sort of looked at it as the way of life I was going to live, like it was fate that had thrown me into this place. I just had to accept it.

"I felt it had become too screwed up for me to get it together, but I knew I was going to die if I kept being an addict. It wasn't an immediate fear of death; it was knowing that I was going to keep on doing this until I died. I saw myself living until 30 or so. Maybe another eight to 10 years. But I also felt a sense of relief. I knew that I had gone so far over the edge that it was going to have to come to an end. I felt maybe things would finally change."

Kim recalls that her treatment at the county jail was kind; however, when her lawyer arranged her release, it was on the condition that she go straight to a detox program. En route she was housed overnight in a larger Nashville jail, where she fell prey to the sexual advances of her jailer.

"In the county jail they were real good to me," she relates. "In fact, the little old jailer felt real sorry for me. I remember him giving me a couple of doses of cough syrup in an attempt to cut the withdrawal. It really didn't do anything, but it was a nice gesture.

"When I got to Nashville, one of the sheriffs tried to feel up my blouse. I hadn't had anything to eat but some chocolate-chip cookies, and I was hungry. He had some hamburgers, and he wanted to feel me up for them. I wouldn't let him, and he got mad and didn't give me the food."

Kim adds that this was not her first, nor her last, experience with men who just assumed a female addict was automatically a coke whore. In the past she had been offered prescriptions in exchange for sexual favors by a lecherous dentist, whom she angered so greatly by turning down that he refused to complete the root canal he had started for her. In the future she would be assigned to a probation officer who also felt some God-given right to make a sexual advance during one of her court-ordered appointments. She requested, and got, a new counselor.

"Men just assume that a woman addict has been sleeping around to get her drugs. I still see a lot of that to this day. It makes me angry, and I jump to the patients' defense. Even in the program the guys hit on the new girls."

On the day following Kim's overnight stay in the Nashville jail her parents drove her to Memphis to check into the mandatory, court-ordered detox program. Kim had refused to go by police escort, and, as always, her parents were more than willing to accommodate her.

The ride was uncomfortable, but "they didn't say anything harsh at all." She was stunned. "I asked them once why they never got angry with me. I told them I was angry because they weren't angry. I said,

'Y'all aren't showing me your true feelings, and I don't feel like you're being honest.'

"They just turned right around and said, 'Well, we're *not* angry. We love you. La-di-da-di-da.' Which I know wasn't the complete truth. The entire time they were the model, caring, loving parents, and I wanted them to be angry at me. But I think that was all borne out of their guilt that they played some part in my addiction.

"I've come to see them as people who had no idea how to handle the drug abuse. Plus, they both came from families that didn't talk about problems. The whole family was in denial. That was just their way of dealing with things. I've never asked them why, but they wouldn't have had an answer for me," she concludes thoughtfully.

"I don't resent it anymore, but I did for a long time. I learned very quickly that I'm responsible for getting better, and with the exception of one or two semiclear moments that I had, I wouldn't have accepted their help. There isn't anything they could have done short of having me committed."

Kim's family did check her into a live-in drug-rehabilitation program that was funded entirely by the United Way. The program was based on A.A.'s 12 Steps to recovery, and so its staff was comprised entirely of recovering addicts.

"It was a really good, strict treatment program. For the first six weeks we couldn't even use the telephone. We had very guarded contact outside of treatment, except for people in Narcotics Anonymous, Cocaine Anonymous, or Alcoholics Anonymous.

"Only [recovering] addicts ran the place, and they knew how manipulative you could be. Our counselors were not trained in psychology, and they didn't have degrees. They could qualify to do the counseling just on staff approval. They didn't waste a lot of time with psychology. You know, 'Why did you end up this way?' or 'Did your mother beat you?' It was more like, 'Okay, it's your job to get out of this fix. What are you going to do now?'

"The program also had the advantage that it was funded; so they were not interested in the money. I see a conflict of interest when a profit motive gets in the way. People act up, but they've got good insurance. The place I went to wouldn't put up with a lot. They said, 'Bye.' Their primary goal was to keep everybody working the program and in a safe environment.

"It was an old house that held 20 people, with a girl's floor and a boy's floor. They didn't let us isolate. We couldn't room alone or go off by ourselves. We did all the household chores and the cooking. I got to be kitchen manager. I planned the menu, bought the food, and assigned people to cook, which was a really scary thing, a big responsibility for me at that time."

Three months later, Kim left the program, and by attending Narcotics Anonymous meetings continued her quest for sobriety. For the first eight months she fought her battle alone while her boyfriend, who had broken probation as a result of this arrest, spent time in a Tennessee workhouse. Kim recognizes that it's a miracle their relationship survived their addictions.

"Today it's not a question of, Do I want to use? But especially in the beginning there were times when, if I hadn't had our future to look forward to and work toward, I might have used again. It might sound corny, but we were just meant to be together."

Kim got a job in a pizza place, made new friends, and after she had been straight for two years, got up the courage to go back to school to fulfill a lifelong dream of becoming a nurse.

"I'd always wanted to do something people-related. Even when I was a little girl, I imagined myself as a missionary or in the Peace Corps or something," she recalls dreamily. "When I decided to go back to school, I had finally begun to believe that things were going to work out. Until then I kept looking for what was going to screw up. I didn't trust success. It was uncomfortable. It wasn't familiar like misery was. But by two years clean I began to believe that this was going to be a long-term thing."

Today Kim is a registered nurse working in a Nashville-based Care Unit, a hospital-based, inpatient addiction-recovery program. Her husband is a carpenter who owns his own business. She feels her past experiences, no matter how hellish, have helped make her the best nurse possible.

"It helps me to accept all lifestyles. I don't prejudge a person. I listen to people and what the patients are telling me. I try to sift it out. I don't just give them a prescription and send them on their way. I love nursing, and because I'm in the program, I'm acutely aware of what these people need."

While her problems have helped her develop a special rapport with her patients, it has not necessarily enhanced her relationship with her co-workers, many of whom maintain a certain distrust of her. Kim refuses to let these prejudices bother her.

"I feel really good about the work I do with patients, regardless of how I feel at times about the staff. I do run into a lot of conflict with other nurses. I believe that they don't trust me as much, because I'm recovering. I think they really believe that it's not a disease, but something morally wrong. I don't feel that from everyone—probably from five out of 15 people.

"But I don't get that from the board of nursing. The people who hired me told me that it didn't matter, and my superiors have shown me that it doesn't matter to them either. The head nurse respects me."

Prior to joining the Care Unit of the hospital, Kim spent her first six months of nursing assigned to its surgical unit, an experience that added a great deal to her nursing skills but proved too stressful and too much of a temptation.

"The surgical staff also knew I was recovering, but it didn't make any difference there, which I felt real good about. They never questioned me. If drugs were missing, I wasn't looked at as the one who did it. I may have been if it were a lot over time or if there were some correlation. I feel the reason for that is that it was so busy, I just jumped right in there and did real good work; so I had credibility.

"But it was a learning experience for me, and it was good. It taught me what painkillers were truly made for. I would see someone come back from surgery screaming and yelling, and I'd give her a shot, and she would get better. I was never really tempted to steal the narcotics, because they're counted, and you have to sign out for them. I knew if I ever did that, my life would be in jeopardy. If the thought even crossed my mind, I would push it out. I spent too long getting to where I was. I'm not ready to be a junkie again.

"But what scared me was that I started thinking about taking sleeping pills. The job was so stressful, and I'd come home at night wired up. Sleeping pills weren't counted, and nobody would miss them. It scared me really bad. I could see myself in a tough state, and I immediately asked for a transfer."

Since becoming sober, Kim has had one other brush with drugs. She had her wisdom teeth out and was given painkillers. Taking those pills both scared and titillated her at the same time. The experience, however, was not what she expected.

"The original prescription was for something like 15 pills. I had them write it for five. I gave the pills to a friend of mine who was not an abuser and who understands me. I was looking forward to that feeling again, without having to feel guilty or like I was using. I only took two because that was all I needed to get over the real bad pain. But it didn't feel anywhere near as wonderful. I thought, 'I wonder why I got hooked on this stuff to begin with?' "

Kim feels that her experiences not only made her a better nurse, but an all-round better human being. It wasn't easy, but her life today made it all worth something.

"I wouldn't want to go through all that again," she concludes. "It wears me out even talking about it. Yet if I had to choose a different life than this, I don't know that I would. My problems taught me at a young age things I could have gone my whole life and not known. First of all I had to decide if I wanted to live or die, and second, who I was, what life was all about, and what did I want out of it all? I love my life today."

LESLIE

LEGAL SECRETARY
CHICAGO, ILLINOIS

Leslie was 25, newly divorced, had a new job, had just moved into the big city, and was living on her own for the first time when one of her few acquaintances introduced her to cocaine. It boosted her confidence and helped salve her emotional turmoil. Within six months of "recreational" use she was addicted. A year and a half later she had a $500-a-day habit. When everything in her life had become "a mess," Leslie, who by then had a live-in boyfriend, quit work and generally dropped out of life. Together they dealt hundreds of thousands of dollars' worth of coke. The situation was nearing a crisis point when her boyfriend's two children from a previous marriage came to live with them. Both Leslie and her lover were suffering toxic reactions to the drug when they finally got help. Today, at age 32 and sober for almost five years, Leslie is happily married and, with a friend, has just opened a design firm.

"I'm from a middle-class family, and I wasn't raised in that environment," she explains. "My mother was a housewife, and my father was a salesman for the steel industry. Neither one of my parents even drank; my dad has an occasional drink. But I'm also adopted. There is the theory that you're genetically predisposed to addiction, but I don't know if my natural parents were addicted.

137

"I didn't really do any drugs in high school; it never really interested me. I did experiment loosely in college—primarily with Ecstasy, mescaline, and pot—but I didn't do it all the time, and it really wasn't a problem. When I left school, I didn't use drugs again; so I had a very limited background with drug usage.

"But then, when I was about 25, I was introduced to cocaine. A friend who's a lawyer knew that I didn't know a lot of people yet; so he just called up and said so-and-so was having a party. Some of the guys there had a half a gram or so and asked, 'Do you want to try it?'

"My friend explained that it didn't make you feel any extremes. He said it didn't make you dopey like Black Beauties, which are like horse tranquilizers; it didn't make you see things like acid; and it didn't make you paranoid like pot—all of which I didn't like. He said it just made you feel *real* good, even better than real good, and that you could stay up later and drink more. So I tried it, and he was right, I really did like it. It made me feel how I wanted to feel because I never liked my real feelings. But my friend never got into it. He used recreationally and never developed a problem. I did."

Part of her attraction to the drug, she now realizes, was its ability to give her confidence. Drastic changes in her life had stressed her out, and coke helped her to cope.

"I had recently separated from my husband and moved to Chicago. I'm from a suburb about 30 miles south of Chicago, and it's a completely different environment. I felt very unsafe in the big city by myself. I had never lived on my own before, nor had I lived in the city.

"I think my emotional state had a lot to do with it. After going through therapy over the years, I now realize I was a perfect kid in high school and college. As my mother says, cocaine was my form of the rebellion I should have gone through when I was a teenager."

It didn't take Leslie long to begin seeking out both the drug and a circle of friends with whom she could use it. Soon she also began drinking heavily to take the nervous edge off the cocaine high.

"I started seeking coke out on weekends real quickly. And when I really started using it, I began drinking like a fish. People couldn't believe the amount of alcohol that I was consuming, whereas before I'd have one or two drinks and that was it.

"I was working at a law firm as a legal secretary. I always ran around a crowd of users, and we started going to parties together. We used to call it Friday-night madness. A group of us would get together and buy just a gram or so and do it and stay up until the wee hours. We'd go to bed and recuperate, and by Sunday we were just fine.

"Eventually, it started to be Friday *and* Saturday nights. Then it started on Thursday, then Wednesday, the natural progression. Pretty soon I was calling into work and making up excuses. I would say I became addicted within six months."

Leslie's increasing drug and alcohol abuse quickly took its toll on her job performance. Whereas she had always been a model employee, she was now falling completely apart, both emotionally and physically.

"I had always been a very, very good employee. I did a lot of overtime and worked for more of the partners than was normal because I was real motivated. Then I started calling into work sick, and, if I did make it after staying up all night, I'd fall asleep in the bathroom or in an empty office and have my girlfriends wake me up.

"I did very detailed work, and it was going down the tubes. I couldn't make phone calls, I couldn't add up figures; I just couldn't do the work. I would schlepp it off to somebody else and say that I was real, real sick. I would tell bizarre lies, like I had cancer or something, to get off the hook. People were real supportive because if you took a look at me, you would have thought something was wrong with me. I'm five two and I was down to about 80 pounds. I was always a mess, always had a cold, and I spent a lot of time in the bathroom. It got to be this cycle.

"Finally, I ran out of excuses and called in and said I had been in a car accident. They were very concerned and called the hospital where I said I was; but I wasn't there. My roommate at the time, who also worked at the firm, called up and said, 'You're in big trouble.' So I called the personnel manager and told her I had a drug problem. She was real supportive, but this was almost five years ago, before a lot of information was out, and I don't think she was really equipped to handle it. What she did was cut out some articles about Cocaine Anonymous and other support groups and left me alone.

"I managed to stay at work a couple more months, but people weren't giving me work anymore, and I was asked to be transferred to another lawyer. No one would take me, and I was asked to leave."

Shortly before she left the law firm, Leslie moved in with the man she had been dating, who was also divorced. John, 35, now sober as

well and married to Leslie, then worked in middle management for
the city of Chicago. He used cocaine rather heavily, and four or five
months before Leslie lost her position he took a leave of absence from
his job to do drugs. Shortly thereafter, he quit altogether and began
dealing. Living together, they both acknowledge, was a crucial turning point in Leslie's addiction.

"I never had a problem prior to cocaine," John reveals. "I never
drank during the week or alcoholically. I smoked pot intermittently
but was never a big pot smoker. When I found coke, it rang my bell in
a big way, and I knew from the start I was going to have a problem.
As long as it was available, I was going to do it. It made me feel
wonderful, and I wanted to replicate that experience.

"When I met Leslie, I was probably buying cocaine twice a
month—weekend usage. But it quickly escalated. Looking back on it,
I think that Leslie, left to her own devices, would never have gotten
involved like she did. She had experimented with it, and that was it.

"Then she met me. Leslie liked me a whole lot, and I liked her. But
if she wanted to hang around with me, I was probably going to be
doing coke. She could hardly hang around with me and not do coke. I
didn't want her if she didn't. I wanted to be around people who were
doing it, and I think she sensed that."

"Right when I moved here, I got involved with John, who kind of
pushed my using along, to be quite honest," Leslie agrees. "He wasn't
dealing at that point, but he got into it very soon after. In fact, the
first time I went out with him, he used, and I didn't know it, because
he didn't think that I used. When he moved in, that's when I really
started using. I even remember thinking, 'This is going to be some
serious using.' "

In the beginning of their relationship cocaine, much lauded as an
aphrodisiac, heightened their sexual contact. But as their addiction
worsened, all their energy was reserved for doing drugs, and their
interest in sex waned altogether. "There is a real sexual side to the
drug," Leslie affirms. "I think everybody has a bit of a sexual hang-
up, and coke releases your inhibitions. In some people I saw it release
them to the extent of no holds barred. I never did that. I stayed with
one partner. But then it kind of turns on you, and you don't want to
have anything to do with sex. It takes too much energy."

It was another five months after she moved in with John before
Leslie's habit reached its peak at $500 a day. She was still maintain-

ing a pretense of normality and had secured another job at a second law firm.

"I was still trying to hold down a job and look respectable. I had never lost a job in my entire life, but I didn't see it, to be quite honest. I thought it was all them. I wondered what was wrong with them. I got a job as a legal secretary to the senior partner of another law firm."

Although her work was just as poor at her second job, again no one really confronted her. By her own choice, however, she remained at the job for only a few months. A year after she began using cocaine, she quit working in order to use full time.

"I was really screwing up. My boss said, 'Your work is really failing.' In fact, I had been there for three weeks, I think, when my boyfriend went down to Florida to make a drug deal. He called up and said, 'I really miss you. Why don't you come down?' I said, 'Fine' and left for a week. I called in and said, 'I'm in Florida, I'll be back soon,' and no one said anything. I got a little bit of a reprimand, but nothing of any importance. I didn't lose my job.

"Finally I went to the guy and said, 'Listen. I have a drug problem.' He sent me to a therapist and then asked me to go to his new job with him when he switched law firms. I looked at him in disbelief and said, 'You've got to be crazy.' I think I felt bad that this guy was being so nice to me, and that's when I quit.

"I justified to myself that I had worked a long time, and it was time to take a break. So I told everyone that I was going to take the summer off and re-evaluate my life and see if I wanted to go back to school to get my MBA or whatever. What I really did was stay home and use drugs."

Leslie and John were doing an extreme amount of cocaine and were both deeply in debt. They were now dealing full time to support not only their drug habit, but also their living expenses. While John handled the majority of the transactions, Leslie jumped in eagerly.

"I had gone through my savings and the money I made when my ex-husband and I sold the house and split the profits. I ran up the maximums on all my credit cards. My bills started catching up to me because I wasn't paying them. I remember one time I didn't have enough money to get to work, and that was early on. I had to ride my bike because I didn't have a dollar for the bus."

Adds John, "I went through whatever cash I had or could put together. About the time things started getting tough, I got into dealing."

"John was the one who made all of the connections and who knew how to get it," Leslie chimes in. "He knew a lot of people in Florida, and he did the big parts. I pretty much stayed at home. But toward the end John was so bad that he couldn't even get up to deal, and I would do it."

"It got to the point where I couldn't function anymore," John explains. "I couldn't even pull it together enough to buy or sell cocaine. I couldn't get off the couch, and I didn't want to leave my house. I didn't want to deal with anyone in any way—not only to deal drugs, but to answer the phone. I was becoming extremely paranoid and kind of emotionally burnt out."

Most men, even male addicts, will look down on a female addict, frequently assuming her to be a coke whore. Leslie, who found more of a stigma attached to herself than John did when they finally sobered up, also encountered that same condescending attitude while dealing.

"What I encountered was the same chauvinistic views that someone would deal with in normal life. They thought they could pull something over on me and that I was an easy target. They didn't think that I knew as much as I did and assumed it would be easier to swindle me because I was a woman. It was really amazing."

Although it's extremely unusual for women to deal coke because of the physical danger involved, Leslie wasn't afraid of the people they dealth with in general, even though some carried guns. "I wasn't really frightened, because, quite honestly, my reality was gone," she confesses. "In that lifestyle your sense of reality and decision making are screwed up. You begin to *think* it's normal. And at the time they didn't seem that scary. The people that we dealt to were pretty normal. Some of them were awful, but the majority were professionals, people you would see and never think they were using. I thought they were pretty okay people because misery loves company. They were my friends. They stayed at our house, or I would go and see them. Now that I look back on it, I'm sure that they were probably some nice people who got screwed up.

"There was one time, though, that I'll never forget. I was sitting in the living room with three women we had met through this whole process, and I realized that all of them were ex-convicts on federal counts. I was very uncomfortable and didn't know how to act. If my mother knew the kind of people that I was mingling with ... *uhhh*."

Leslie became paranoid that they would be busted, but John rarely worried about that. Ironically, the closest they came to being arrested was when Leslie's parents, out of a feeling of helplessness in the face of their child's addiction, nearly called the police.

"In the beginning I was selling to people who were my friends or friends of friends," John recounts. "It was real innocuous the way it developed. Coupled with the fact that psychologically it made me feel terrific so that if I had any insecurities, they were gone when I was doing coke. I was confident, relaxed, and cool. It was easy to sweep away fears. I didn't know anybody getting busted for cocaine. You read about it in the paper, but nobody I knew was having any big difficulty.

"But toward the end I was worried. In the beginning it was a little thing, $300–$400–$500 worth of cocaine. Toward the end Leslie and I were dealing a bunch of coke, maybe $60–$80–$100,000 worth. I was going to Florida frequently and picking up kilos. It's a miracle we never got busted."

"I was scared for John when he was going down there, and I started getting paranoid that we'd get busted. My parents were so perplexed about what was going on. They apparently knew and thought seriously about calling the police because I was so unreachable. I'm very glad that they didn't, because that really wouldn't have solved anything."

Though Leslie's parents never interceded, it was obvious that Leslie and John had a serious problem. "I'm very close to my parents, and I wasn't seeing them at all. I wasn't speaking to them, and I wasn't in contact with any of my friends. We literally missed a Christmas party one year. We were either too high or fell asleep. We were always late for things, sometimes an entire day late. We would make the commitment with all good intentions and just never follow through. I remember one time they had a birthday party for my mother at a real nice restaurant. We showed up and were so high. We sat down, ordered all this liquor, threw the present at her, didn't eat, and just bolted.

"I think they were just afraid to break off the final string. And they were too embarrassed to ask for help or what to do. They were really afraid if they approached me and said anything that the one thin sliver they had open would be gone, and they would lose me forever. They thought some kind of connection was better than nothing."

In the midst of this downward spiral John's two children, who were having problems with their mother, came to live with him. It didn't take long for Cindy, then 16, and John Jr. (Johnny), then 14, to realize that something was seriously wrong.

"I pretty much knew things weren't right before I came into the situation," reveals John Jr., now 19 and working in construction. "I hadn't been informed, but visiting on weekends, I started noticing, 'Hey, this doesn't seem right.' Maybe I'd see some paraphernalia around or something. But I really didn't know the extent of the problem until I moved in."

In fact, unable to control their addiction, John and Leslie sat the two teenagers down and forewarned them. Sighs Leslie, "We told them right away when they came to live with us. We felt we couldn't hide it. It was not open for discussion, but they needed to know that it was going on. We told them, 'This is what we do, this is what the people are here for, and you can't bring over any friends.' "

"When I first arrived," recalls Cindy, now 20 and a psychology major at an Illinois university, "it was late at night, and Leslie greeted me. She told me my dad had just gone to bed. I didn't know what was going on with cocaine or anything, but I was hurt that he didn't want to see me. I found out later that my dad didn't want to face reality. He was so nervous, he went upstairs and couldn't see me. It was a shock that his kids had come to live with him because it was a decision made really fast. We were going through a lot of problems with puberty or something, and we were driving my mom up the wall.

"My mom didn't use drugs or alcohol, but I had experimented. I would drink with my friends at high school and stuff like that, but I had never used cocaine. My first reaction was that I felt pretty mature my dad was telling me this. He was really straightforward with us. I felt really respected. I wasn't frightened, because I had looked up to my dad my whole life—until I saw exactly what their living style was like and what they were doing.

"Also, my dad's 40 now, and I'm 20. We're kind of close in age, so my parents have always been 'with it.' They weren't like older parents who were from another generation. So I thought it was kinda cool."

Both kids concede it didn't take long for them to realize that their father and Leslie's drug use was not cool. It was devastating.

"I saw how angry they got," Cindy laments, "and their mood swings. Sometimes they would be just partying and real happy, and then I would see them come down real hard, and they would fight. We were never abused, and I wasn't frightened; but if I thought my dad was coming down and in a bad mood, I would just steer clear."

While the children were never abused, they were not properly cared for, and the emotional upheaval was constant. In fact, there was a role reversal, and Cindy and Johnny began caring for their parents.

"They started taking care of us," Leslie admits. "They would screen the calls, do the laundry, and pick up the house. They handled a lot of the grocery shopping. But they never beat us up about it, saying, 'You're nothing but a bunch of drug addicts' or anything like that. They tried to keep us in some semblance of a family unit as much as possible. They showed us in a lot of ways that we weren't responsible for us anymore."

Although they felt bad about the situation that the kids were forced to endure, Leslie points out that there wasn't another choice at the time. "They had come from a situation that I think wasn't much better, even though there weren't drugs involved. There weren't many options. They didn't have anywhere else to go; so what could they do but say okay?"

"Our house was in no order," Cindy complains. "Sometimes Leslie would really get on top of things and clean and go to the grocery store. And other times the house would be upside down for a week. My brother and I basically took care of things ourselves. It got to a point where they wouldn't even leave the house that much.

"I'd come home from school and my dad would just be waking up. I hated that. Everything was so out of order. Then it got to really scare me because I saw how much cocaine was controlling my dad and Leslie."

John regrets that period in their lives and feels responsible for the plight of the entire family. "I look back on those times and Leslie trying to make a stable, healthy home for those kids in the midst of what we were involved in. I loved her for what she was trying to do, and I was dragging her down. And the kids, despite her best effort, knew what was going on. We were both just spiraling down, and I felt terrible. I felt worse about dragging Leslie down than I did about myself or the kids seeing me in that situation. I knew that she wouldn't be where she was if it weren't for me."

Though they were using heavily, they did not use in front of the children, either hiding in the bedroom or sending them out for a while.

"They didn't want to expose us directly to it," Cindy acknowledges. "Sometimes when my brother and I went to do laundry, there were seven bags, and it was an all-day project at the Laundromat. I remember once when my brother kept saying, 'These clothes aren't dirty.' They just wanted us to stay there a little longer so they could party, because they didn't use cocaine in front of us."

"My dad always sent us out," John Jr. adds, "and he didn't have a lot of people stopping by. If he had to do something, he'd leave. I never really saw strange-looking characters coming up to the house and knocking on the door or anything. It was not for my eyes; I was out. My dad had this problem, and we were going to see it in certain ways, but there were certain things we weren't going to see. That was one of them."

"We would always tell them to leave the house and give them money," Leslie confirms. "They knew what we were doing, but we tried to make it seem normal. They would go to school, and we would try our darndest to get up by the time they came home.

"I tried to do things I enjoyed, like needlepoint, but it would turn into a mess. Anything that I did was a mess. I didn't drive; I hardly ever went out after a while," Leslie reveals sadly. "I didn't need to—I ordered everything in. It was just too much trouble, and I had to worry about where I would do my cocaine. But you keep rationalizing it, 'Oh, when the summer's over, I'll stop this.' "

As their living situation worsened, so did the children's behavior. Unsupervised and overly curious about the drug that was running their lives, both kids experimented with their parents' stash. Cindy hated cocaine's effect, but Johnny began using it on a semiregular basis.

Says Cindy, "After a while my curiosity got me, and I really wanted to see what it was like. They left the house to go to a bar or something, and my brother and I went to their room, looked for it, and took a really small amount and snorted it. I didn't like it at all. It hit me immediately and was a big shock. I tasted lots of icky things in my throat and got real nervous. Mostly I was scared that my dad would find out. Even though he was using, we still respected his authority as a parent."

"I didn't know that much about cocaine," says John Jr., "but I was curious. I would go and snitch some, just once in a while at first— maybe every week or so. Then I started seeing the toll it was taking on my parents. I quit because they quit, but I don't think I would have continued."

Both kids isolated themselves, refusing to confide their problems to friends, family members, or counselors. Their best friends were each other.

"I was embarrassed," Cindy admits. "I didn't want to hear any judgments. I knew that people would talk bad about my parents, and I didn't really trust anybody, not even the counselor at school. I felt people would think they were real lowlifes if they knew what was going on. I just talked to my brother. We were really close throughout the entire thing and stuck together."

Not only had Leslie and John's life become a mess by this time, their health was nearly ruined. "My gums bled a lot; I was losing hair," recounts Leslie. "I ended up perforating my septum, although I had stopped using already when I found out about it. I had to have a five-hour operation to get a rebuilt nose, which will always be a problem for me. But you don't really believe that there's anything wrong. I think I would look in the mirror and see somebody I *used* to be. Toward the end I got up to 150 pounds because I was drinking so heavily. The joke was that I was the only fat cocaine addict who ever went into treatment.

"John was pretty much toxic. He was sweating a lot and getting extreme headaches. We were fighting a lot. We started thinking, 'We can't live like this anymore.'"

Leslie wanted to stop and knew that she would die if she didn't, but she was entirely out of control. Several times, out of desperation, she considered suicide. More often she tried to run away from reality.

"They were kind of half-assed attempts. One time I took a steak knife and tried to slit my wrists. I cut myself a little bit, but not to any degree. It really shocked me that I was even attempting that, and I stopped myself. Another time I thought about jumping out a window.

"I *was* killing myself though. I would run away and sit in a movie house for 14 hours, thinking, 'Okay, I'm not going to do coke.' Then

I'd go home and have it right there. John's father had a summer home in another state. I'd run away and go there for a couple of days. But by the second day I'd be climbing the walls, saying, 'I've got to have it.'

"People said I was the worst user they'd ever spent time with because I had become so depressed and paranoid. I wasn't any fun anymore. John was fun. But basically, we were just lying in bed doing drugs. We couldn't get up in the morning without it. Somebody once asked me, 'When you did a line, what size was it?' Well, we never did one, because all we had was a bag that we just continually scooped from."

Though they had both freebased, the most addictive form of cocaine use, they preferred snorting. Leslie just didn't like to smoke cocaine, but John had a more insidious reason.

Relates Leslie, "I didn't like it, because freebasing really isolates you—even more than snorting—in my opinion. It's because the high is so intense that you can't even talk, and you're just zoned-out. And the process of preparing it is so focused that no one talks. Freebasing wasn't social, and it took any element of so-called fun out of it."

"We 'based intermittently," John adds, "but I wanted to do coke all the time; so that ruled out 'basing as a consistent way of getting high. The last six to eight months, if we were awake, we were doing coke. I'm talking about doing a line before you put your feet on the floor in the morning. But it wasn't morning, it was more like afternoon. And you can't 'base all the time. You can't 'base if you're in the car or a bar or during the course of your day, because of the paraphernalia and apparatus. I've certainly done my fair share of 'basing, but 90 percent of my cocaine use was snorting. I mean, witness Leslie's nose and mine."

"I remember one time at the end, after a night of using, I couldn't get any more cocaine up my nose from pain," says Leslie, who seems embarrassed at the recollection. "I couldn't sleep, and I was real cranky; so I went downstairs and sat there with my cocaine, my bottle of scotch, and a bowl under my nose because it was just continuously bleeding. I would sit there and try to stuff the cocaine up and then think, 'Oh, no, I shouldn't be doing this; I want to go to sleep.' Then I'd take a slug of scotch out of the bottle. That's how pathetic things were, and that's the picture I used to remember when I was getting clean."

Leslie once went for help, even going so far as to call her parents from the clinic, admit she was an addict, and tell them that she was checking into rehabilitation; however, the inconsiderate treatment she received prior to check-in made her leave.

"I didn't like how I was handled; so I left after about three hours. They were harsh and very concerned about payment. I was sitting there, and I had been up for about three days. My nose was bleeding, and you could tell that I was both a physical and emotional wreck. Even though I was high, they made me wait, and they were rude. I mean, if somebody comes to that point in their life and they're asking for help, you should be a little nicer to them. Maybe that's an excuse I was using at the time. I think part of it is and part isn't."

A few months later John checked into a newly formed, inpatient program called Lifeline for 10 days. Leslie, convinced this was their new start and she could quit on her own, cleared the house of drugs. She then went out and landed a job as a secretary in a large public-relations agency. Their effort was short-lived.

"John said, 'This is it. We're going to clean up our lives.' I was really happy about it, and I sold the coke. I wasn't going to flush it, because we needed the money if we weren't going to deal anymore. I didn't find religion or anything; I was very practical. But I didn't enter treatment, because we didn't have the insurance, and I thought I didn't need it. I have a hard time asking for help, period, sober or not.

"I do remember both of us lying in bed, and John saying, 'We're not going to live like this anymore. Things will get better.' And I would look at him and go, 'Right,' because I didn't think that they would. We lasted six weeks."

Almost immediately, Leslie began faltering at work, but again no one approached her. Although it had not been her intent when she landed the job, she now had the insurance to seek help.

"It's unbelievable that nobody said anything to me. They think they're being polite, but oh, my God, they're not! The one thing that really pushed us to look at what was going on was that my boyfriend's best friend, whom he had known since he was six years old, came down one night when I wasn't around. I was probably hiding out at the movie theater or something. And he said, 'What are you doing? You are really screwing up your life!' He read John the riot act, and it really had an effect.

"I got into treatment, and John went right after I did. It was real difficult for me. I went in and literally said, 'I want my own room, a TV, and visitation with my dog.' I was a real princess. Here I was with all these people, and I thought, 'Hurumph, they're drug addicts.' Needless to say, I got turned around quickly enough.

"Despite the physical withdrawal, it was a relief. My body had been so beaten up, it was just grateful that no drugs or alcohol were being put into it. But the psychological withdrawal heavily tormented me for a year. I just wanted it and didn't understand why I couldn't have it and all those good feelings that I had in the beginning. That's very hard to replace. You don't really get those feelings out of normal, everyday life."

Leslie chose Lifeline, a 28-day inpatient treatment facility with a two-year After Care follow-up program because she initially needed to remove herself from her drug-ridden lifestyle entirely. "You really need to get out of your environment," she stresses. "I mean, the day I got out of treatment, a so-called friend showed up with coke."

After rehab, the stress of cleaning up the mess they had made out of their lives during years of using added to the nagging torment.

"When you get off drugs, it is so overwhelming to see the mess you've created," Leslie continues. "The frustration of cleaning up things, talking to people, making new friends, and making amends was awful. Plus, you have to start doing all the things that you didn't do while using. Like we had no furniture, we hadn't gone to the dentist or paid our car payments.

"I had to file bankruptcy for $20,000, and that was just me. It's real difficult to write somebody and say, 'I'm going to pay you $10 a month for the rest of my natural life practically to pay you off.'

"I don't think my parents believed for two years that I was really going to show up if I said I was or if I had a cold that I *really* had a cold. My mom will say, 'Now, you're not going to, are you?' I also had that reaction with John when he got clean. If he didn't come home when he was supposed to, I got so nervous."

Leslie returned to the public relations agency after six weeks in treatment but found the prejudice against female addicts almost overwhelming. "They can't fire you if go into drug rehabilitation," she explains. Federal law prohibits your employer from firing you if you have sought help. But they were very, very angry. I had only been there for a short period of time, and I didn't want to go back. I was embarrassed. I had been gone for six weeks, and some people knew. But I really felt I had to make a go of it.

"When I went back, my same position wasn't there, and I didn't have work for a while. I just sat there. I think they were hoping to get me to quit. I did end up getting a couple of bosses who were terrific and was promoted out of the secretarial role. But I reached a dead end because one of the people on the executive committee didn't feel the company should reward a drug addict.

"I think most people, including me before all this happened, if asked, 'Who would you think of as a drug addict?' wouldn't think of a female. Therefore you're really strange if you do turn into one—especially when you're a woman who's gotten her degree from a good college, who's had a proper upbringing and a good family. It's almost like, 'How dare you? You have no right to be doing that!' "

Leslie, in her next position, worked six months on the options exchange, wanting to be a stockbroker, but found the hectic pace encouraged compulsiveness and drug use among many of her coworkers. She left. Recently, she and a friend opened a new company.

"My degree was in fashion design, and I come from an artistically creative family. I do design work. The company is just four months old, but it's going fairly well and we're very hopeful."

And despite the fact that her counselors in drug rehabilitation predicted her relationship with John would end, the couple have now been happily married for 2½ years. Today John works as a manager for Lifeline, the program that helped them achieve sobriety.

"When I went into treatment," Leslie thinks back, "I was told there was a pretty good chance that we wouldn't make it—number one because we'd have a hard time breaking the habit. They tell you not to go to places where you used. Well, we used all over, 24 hours a day. Plus, we had to stop dealing. That was a lot of money. It made you feel powerful, and it was an easy way to make a living. We waited awhile to get married. We wanted to make sure everything was going to settle down.

"But in some ways I'm really glad that we went through this to-gether because now I don't think there's anything that we couldn't go through. I can't imagine anything else being that awful."

"Our relationship was one in a million," John smiles. "We're both real grateful. We had little lucid glimpses that there was some real stuff here worth saving. We were fortunate to be able to keep it to-gether. It's wonderful."

Today John feels particularly rewarded by his work with Lifeline, and Leslie has done some volunteer work with the program. They both continue private therapy and attend meetings of Cocaine Anony-mous. And not only have Cindy and John Jr. gone through family therapy with their parents, but they have both developed strong anti-drug opinions.

"I've experienced things very few of my friends have," Cindy real-izes, "and I've seen a lot that they haven't seen. It did make me grow up a little faster, but I don't think I'm damaged by it. I'm proud of my father and Leslie, that they came out of it, and that I have such a good relationship with them now. I don't really feel damaged by what our relationship was like when they were using. I'm actually glad that I've gone through all this; so I won't let it happen to me."

"I've seen the worst, and it scares me," John Jr. agrees. "I think drugs are no good. They're real attractive to newcomers, they've got a real good hold on a lot of people, and they're really screwing up the economy."

"The kids are a lot wiser," says John, almost apologetically. "They're a lot less apt to bullshit themselves about the toll drugs can take on someone, because they've seen it. Will I sit here and say that means they'll never acquire a drug problem? I wouldn't say that. They won't go into anything naively, but that doesn't mean they won't go into anything. The verdict is still out. But at the moment we're just back to normal, pain-in-the-ass parent/kids stuff."

The entire family has come a long way, but it is still easy for Leslie to recall the nightmare they were once living. "I don't remember the good times. And in some ways it's still an embarrassment. But it was just so easy to get into, and it was complete and total obsession. I mean, there was nothing else. I would have kept going until I died."

CATHY AND TAMI

TEENAGERS
SOUTHERN CALIFORNIA

Cathy, now 29, and Tami, now 26, were born in Ogden, Utah, but moved to southern California as young children. In their early teens they began drinking to cope with a severely dysfunctional family life. Their mother was a staunch pillar of the community, and the entire family belonged to the Mormon church—a religion so strict that it even forbids the consumption of caffeine. But the girls' mother had a secret. She was also a practicing alcoholic who brought home a succession of men and who began abusing her children as her disease progressed. Both girls, as well as two younger brothers, became alcoholic/ addicts. Today the entire family is sober. Each of the girls bottomed out on cocaine use but attained sobriety before the disease took them to the depths some addicts reach. They both functioned "normally" in their day-to-day dealings, an accomplishment that many addicts use to deny they have a problem. While thankful, they are quick to point out that their disease morally destroyed them all. This is the story of a contemporary family in distress, as seen through the eyes of three people with very different perspectives.

"My mother was a practicing alcoholic; so I was the mom," laments Cathy. "I was the oldest, and I shouldered all the responsibility. My friends' mothers were always closer to me than my own. I used to call them all Mom."

"At the age of eight, right after my father died, I learned to hide my feelings. My first recollection of getting high on a substance was with food. That was my first addiction, and the relationship was so exciting. I would go visit my grandparents, my father's parents, on weekends. They would take me to the grocery store and buy me whatever I wanted to eat, which consisted of cookies, ice cream, chocolate pudding, anything sugary. I remember sitting in the backseat of the car just anticipating getting home and not knowing what I was going to eat first. I was really into it.

"Personally, I believe the first time an addict gets high, we spend the rest of our lives trying to recapture that feeling. That was my first high, and I spent the rest of my life, up until the time I got sober, trying to recapture that. Years later, when I did cocaine, that was the high I was looking for."

Cathy was 13 or so when her mother began to drink more heavily. Her sister Tami was ten; her little brothers were five and two. Cathy began drinking in high school but limited it; so she was able to care for the house and her siblings.

"I would drink on weekends, and that was about it. But when I drank, I would drink to get totally drunk. And of course I ate along with it."

Although the family was active in the Mormon church, which strictly forbids consumption of any substance harmful to the body, including caffeine, Cathy was able to push her convictions aside. "I held offices and was very well respected in the church, but my big secret was that my mother drank and that I did too. I would drink on Friday and Saturday nights and then get up and go to church on Sunday mornings and participate in the services like nothing had happened. I started to drink in high school because I wanted to fit in so badly. I would have done anything, even if it went against everything I believed in."

Tami had never felt a connection to the church and attended only because her mother, Anne, insisted. After Anne's third divorce, from a Mormon man who adopted her two daughters and fathered her two sons, she basically "renounced" the church, according to her daughters. It was then that their mother's drinking began to escalate.

"I suppose it's similar to going to Alcoholics Anonymous," Anne says. "When you stop going to meetings, you relapse. When I stopped being active in the church, my thoughts tended to go another way. The church wasn't giving me what I was seeking or needed. Alcohol did."

The girls had easy access to liquor. Their mother was a successful real estate agent, selling more than $1 million in property a year. She also ran for election to the local city council and served nine years as a reserve deputy sheriff. She entertained frequently and kept refreshments handy.

"My mother loved to entertain," relates Cathy. "She's a very driven, successful woman and very well known in the community. So people were constantly dropping by. There was booze in the refrigerator and a fully stocked bar in the living room at all times. That's how my sister started drinking."

"I was in the seventh or eighth grade when I started smoking pot, probably on a daily basis," Tami admits. "It felt absolutely wonderful. I hung around with people who sold it. I had a girlfriend whose mother smoked dope and another friend whose mother grew it. We used to steal some.

"Shortly thereafter I took my first drink. It was Jack Daniels, and it was right out of the bottle. I don't even remember if I got drunk, just that it burned going down. I replaced it with water, and Mom never knew. I was angry at my mom for being the way she was. I was angry that I had to take care of her kids. I was angry because she never came home when she said she would. I drank to numb the feelings, to be somebody."

Although Tami doesn't remember some of her early actions, Cathy recalls one behavior pattern quite vividly. "My sister used to get up in the mornings after a party and go drink the empties— glasses around the house that had cigarette butts in them and a little liquor left. She would finish them off and then go out to the trash cans in the back of the house and drink what was left in the beer bottles."

"I wasn't a teenage alcoholic that took a thermos filled with alcohol to school," Tami counters, "but I'd get loaded before school. First period was driver's education, and that's how I learned to drive— loaded. I'd go home before third period, and we'd smoke some joints. I started to black out when I was 17 or 18. In my sophomore or junior year I was there two out of nine weeks, and nobody ever said a thing to me.

"I got stopped one time when I was 17 years old for an open container, and the cop let me go. I should have had dozens of 502s [arrests for drunk driving], but nobody ever did anything to me. I really wish that someone other than me would have realized something was wrong."

Both women remember receiving the same admonishment from their mother against drugs; however, alcohol wasn't included in that warning. "My mother told me that if I smoked pot, I would do heroin," Cathy says. "I was not interested in becoming a junkie, but I figured drinking was okay."

"I believe that today," adds Tami. "Pot does lead to bigger and better drugs, like cocaine. But at the time I thought, 'No way.' I remember my mom let me have a party one New Year's Eve, and she let us drink champagne that night. I thought I was the coolest thing that walked the earth because my mom let me drink. But mostly I did a lot of drinking by myself."

Cathy did not drink heavily until college and was a graduate before she tried cocaine. But Tami's addiction progressed much more quickly than her older sister's did. As a sophomore in high school she was using hard drugs, specifically amphetamines.

"A girlfriend introduced me to crank, crystal Methedrine. Her boyfriend sold it, and he initially gave it to us because we cleaned his house. It's similar to cocaine. You snort it. But it burns more, and it has a better high than cocaine.

"I remember Fourth of July one year, I had done probably eight lines. My heart felt like it was going to jump out of my skin, and I went swimming in the ocean by myself at two in the morning. I liked my heart pounding. I don't know why. Maybe it was because as a child my life was so much like that. There were times I'd just lie in bed and wonder what was going to happen when my mom got home. But my friend's boyfriend pulled us off the crank because he could tell how hooked we were."

As their mother's drinking worsened, so did her treatment of her children. She became physically and emotionally abusive and frequently left them alone for long periods of time.

"I can remember being yanked out of bed at three o'clock in the morning," Cathy says, "because one fork was not clean and my mom was in a drunken stupor. And I'd have to wash every dish in the kitchen. If I had been cleaning house all day and she came home at night and there was one load of laundry that wasn't done, it totally discounted everything else."

The same punishment was meted out for Tami after Cathy left the bedlam to attend college. Once at school, Cathy wanted as little interaction with her family as possible, and the burdens fell on Tami's shoulders.

"It was a combination of physical and emotional abuse. Also neglect," Tami observes. "Physically, in the sense that she graduated from her hand to extension cords to leather dog leashes and hairbrushes. I remember the wooden spoon most. And the look on her face. She never spoke if she was angry. I don't think she ever really yelled, but she would look at me, and her look said, 'You piece of shit.' She never really said that, but that's the way I looked at it.

"There was one incident in particular when she was mad, and she pulled me out of bed at two o'clock in the morning and starting banging my head against the headboard. If I remember, it was because the dishwasher wasn't on. Her boyfriend had to stop her. They were both really drunk; I could smell the liquor.

"I went to my stepdad's house that night, and he said, 'Just go to sleep. It will all be better tomorrow.' Nobody ever said, 'There's a problem.' I don't know if it was sick people through sick eyes or if my mom was so successful [at her job] that they really didn't think it could be that bad. I used to go to school feeling really sorry for myself, and I'm learning today that I had every right to."

Cathy believes that perfectionism is a common trait among addicts who are seeking some control in their lives. While she resented her treatment as a child, she can identify the same trait in her own behavior today.

"We want to control things, and perfectionism is a control issue. It's also a quirk of mine. I expect that my roommate will remember to turn off the lights. I want everything in its place. In the kitchen I want the canisters right where I leave them. I know if someone has had some of my salad dressing in the refrigerator or if the bottle is moved. I know if someone has been in my room just by the way the bed looks."

Their mother readily admits to being a perfectionist, but she does not recall her behavior in the same light as her children. Anne, who was abandoned as a child and who lived in a series of foster homes, felt she was simply trying to give her children the things she never had, which included love. With few communication skills she often tried to buy her children's affection.

"I guess I am a perfectionist, and things weren't done the way I wanted," Anne admits now. "But I really don't recall those times at all. Only recently did it come to me that I was beginning to be an abusive mother. Any mother loses her temper, but I could be a machete-mouth, saying things that shouldn't have been said. At the time I thought I was being a normal parent because that's what I got when I was a kid—willow switches, rulers, belts, and things like that. I saw nothing wrong with it then. Today I would characterize it as child abuse.

"But my children were the most important thing in the world to me. I loved them the most. Basically, because of how deeply I loved them, I never followed through with my thoughts of suicide. I don't think I could have given them any more love. That was the thing that I was starved for when I was growing up, the love of my parents and my mother. I never remember my mother telling me that she loved me. I thought I told my kids I loved them all the time. But it's entirely possible that could be my perception of it.

"I also showed them by providing a nice home and toys. I used to tell myself, 'It's not the quantity of time you spend with your children, it's the quality of time.' Therefore, I rationalized, I could work two jobs and give my kids everything that I never had. I thought I was going to do everything differently.'"

Her children don't recall her ever telling them that she loved them. They do remember calling her at the bar and begging her to come home, to no avail.

"I think my mom is in a lot of denial about what it was really like," Cathy huffs. "My mom was a blackout drinker, and I don't think that she remembers a lot of what really went on. I had a brand-new BMW when I was a junior in high school. I was given material things all the time, but I was pretty miserable for most of my life. I just didn't know it until I got sober and looked back on it. The reality is that I was an abused child, and I'm just learning about that."

"When I was 13," Tami says quietly, "I remember holding a dull razor blade up to my wrists. I don't know why I didn't do it. I think because I didn't want to go through the physical pain. But I wanted to die, and I wanted them to feel really sorry for me. I thought, 'Now they'll really care about me,' and 'Maybe they'll miss me now.' I was an attention-starved kid.

"We used to call her at the bar and ask her to come home, and she'd say, 'I'll be there in an hour.' But she wouldn't come for three, four, five hours. It used to really piss me off."

"I intended to go home after just one more drink," Anne explains. "I can remember them calling just as clear as day. I'd say, 'Well, so-and-so just walked in. Let me say hi to him, and I'll be on my way in a few minutes.' As much as I wanted to go home and be with them, the power of alcohol, the power of belonging to a clique, was so strong that it overcame my going to be with my children. They mothered one another.

"I wasn't doing anything that anybody else of my stature wasn't doing. I loved going to bars, and I loved dancing. I let men pick me up anytime they showed any type of affection for me. I was so hungry for love and attention. Alcohol made me lose my morals. But I wasn't always as bad as I got at the end."

It was a three-day binge that left her two sons, ages 15 and 12, alone at home that finally brought Anne to her senses and led her to Alcoholics Anonymous for help. "I don't exactly recall when it was, but there was a time I passed over that invisible line into chronic alcoholism and blackouts."

Although she had blacked out and only knows about the incident from her daughter, she points it out as an example of how far she had gone. She recounts taking Cathy, then in college, to New York City at Christmastime. The two of them went on a drinking binge, then caught a limo. Anne thought the driver was in the wrong end of town, pulled a small revolver from her purse, and threatened to blow his head off if he didn't return them to the hotel.

"I started losing my car and my purse all the time," she reveals. "I was thrown out of the exclusive bar I used to go to because I hit one guy over the head with my purse. I found myself starting out the evening at the yacht club and ending up at a sleazy bar downtown and feeling that was where I belonged.

"I thought it was the type of liquor I was drinking; so I switched from scotch to brandy. I thought it was cheap wine; so I drank expensive wines. Then I thought it was my age. I'm getting older, and my metabolism is different.

"But on my 47th birthday, when I left the kids at home alone and went off for a couple of days to Catalina Island, that's when I realized that something was drastically wrong. Every time I came home, I was so remorseful, so guilty and ashamed. I loved these kids the most, and my life was going to hell in a hand basket. But my last drunk was not my worst. I had hit lots of bottoms."

Anne drank the last two Heinekens in the refrigerator, called Alcoholics Anonymous, and hasn't stopped attending since. She has been sober since 1983.

When Cathy went away to a junior college, it was a Mormon school, and her drinking halted abruptly. Eventually, however, she attended a larger university and located a group of people who broke all the rules.

"Drugs and alcohol were totally taboo at the first school I attended, and I didn't drink or use, but I ate. Again, I wanted to fit in. I was willing to do whatever it was that the people around me were doing, and at that time it was not drinking and using. I left there and went to Brigham Young University, where I found a group of people who drank. One more time I wanted to be accepted, and that's where I learned how to *really* drink. In my mind there was something about having a drink in your hand that meant you were grown up."

At home and in her senior year of high school, Tami became pregnant. She dropped out of school and began working in fast-food restaurants. Her mother asked her to move out. Tami and her boyfriend, whom she met at age 13 and who later became her husband, moved in together. After a while they began sharing an apartment with a friend who happened to deal hashish. The roommate later began dealing cocaine.

"I could've continued to go to school, I suppose, but my dream was to have a house with a white picket fence and a couple of dogs and a kid" Tami says today. "When I realized that wasn't happening, I decided to end the pregnancy. It was almost five months. We stayed up all night crying about it.

"Then we moved in with this guy who started to deal cocaine, and it really started to go downhill from there. He got it from a guy who baked it. It was called 'repo cocaine.' It's cut with other substances and preprocessed to be more economical. We used to go to his house, where he was pulling it out of the ovens. I have no idea what it was, but it felt good. We hardly ever had to pay for it. We did anything—from nothing to an eighth of an ounce a week. I did whatever was available, whenever I got it."

While Tami can't bring to mind her very first experience with cocaine, she recalls quite vividly how it made her feel. Even today her description is almost rapturous.

"It was just sort of like magic. It helped me talk to people, and it gave me a feeling of being somebody that I wanted to be. If I needed to be sexy, it made me sexy. Whatever I needed to be, it made me. It gave me a feeling of being superior. I guess it was an illusion, but it felt real. And it never really let me down.

"You could probably call me a garbage junkie. I'd do anything, but cocaine and alcohol were my major choices. I liked the combination. The booze would bring me down a little so I could do more cocaine, and it helped take the edge off the withdrawal. I'd lay there and drink a beer like a baby bottle to pass out. I was looking for oblivion because I hated how I felt when I came down. There was such an intense craving and need for it. The hangovers I got when I mixed cocaine and alcohol were incredibly painful, just paralyzing. But I figured if I drank in the morning, I was an alcoholic. I did drink at lunch sometimes.

"Toward the end it was a vicious circle. I'd get hold of some coke, and I'd say, 'I'll only do one line, just one line.' But it was never, ever, ever, just one line. It always led to many, many more."

At 19 Tami finally married her childhood sweetheart, and at age 20 she had a daughter. She drank very little during her pregnancy and used almost no drugs. But to compensate, like her sister, she began to overeat.

"I did coke once during my first trimester, and it made me ill. I felt so guilty. I would have blown my brains out rather than do it again. It was the worst thing you could ever do to a child. I drank an occasional wine, and I substituted food. I binged, and I gained 100 pounds. I developed gestational diabetes."

Like her mother, Tami also was beginning to show signs of violence. "I became very violent toward my husband at a party one time. He told me not to go into a room—we both knew they were doing coke in there—and I hit him. I felt so remorseful."

But there were other incidents. "We'd put the kid to bed when we got home from work and start partying at seven o'clock at night. One time when she was six months old, I started to get very angry at her for crying, for interfering with my partying. She wouldn't go to sleep, and it just pissed me off; so I started to shake her.

"My husband would tell me to get up and take care of the baby, but I couldn't get off the couch. After a hangover my head felt like it weighed 500 pounds. I really don't know why he never said, 'I'm sick of this.' I think he may have been in denial himself."

A series of events led to Tami's sobriety. Her drinking reached a point that was definitely not social; she became extremely paranoid and was unable to function normally. Finally, her husband, who had never pursued drugs with Tami's enthusiasm, although he did use recreationally, shocked her sober. Shortly thereafter he also stopped using drugs altogether.

"As my disease progressed, when I had company over to my house, I would collect all the glasses and save them," Tami says shamefully. "I never threw anything down the drain, because I knew that I would need it later. One time my husband heard me clanging around in the kitchen while I was fishing beer bottles out of the garbage. He asked what I was doing, and I said I was cleaning out the cupboards. It was three o'clock in the morning. It wasn't social drinking, but I didn't know that.

"I was afraid to ever leave my house. I wouldn't go to the mailbox. I remember one time, just after I got married, the gardeners came to do the lawns in our apartment complex, and I was so afraid of them, I hid behind my kitchen counter and peeked at them. I just had extreme paranoia, and I still suffered from it two years into sobriety.

"It was a chain of events that helped me realize I had a problem. But once, when we were in Las Vegas, I was really drunk, and my husband said to me, 'You look just like your mom, that look.' And I knew the look he was talking about because I hated that look, and it just crushed me. I absolutely never wanted to be a drunk like her."

In the meantime Cathy had finished college and secured a job in Los Angeles managing a store for a luggage manufacturer. She was quite successful and was eventually responsible for six stores throughout the state, which required her to travel extensively. It was an employee who first introduced her to cocaine.

"I thought that I had a handle on my life. I had a great job, and I was doing things that most people dream about. I was living in the fast lane, and I thought I had arrived.

"Drugs happened purely by accident. I was very attracted to a man who was working for me, who happened to be gay and I didn't know it. I wanted to have more of a relationship with him. I was begging him to teach me how to do coke because I wanted to fit in one more time.

"He brought some into my office, put it out on the desk, and taught me what to do with it. I remember snorting it and thinking, 'Gosh, what's all the hype about? This is no big deal.' After about 10 minutes my face was buried in it, trying to get high off it, because it just didn't seem like it was working. The reality of it was that it was working really well, and I loved it. I began a pretty heavy love affair with the drug.

"I was doing a gram to a gram and a half a day. I always carried it with me. I had a little bag I carried that had a mirror and a straw—separate from everything else. I'd go into my office, lock the door, and snort it up. They I'd go back out on the floor and work with the customers.

"I also drank every day. I didn't drink in the morning, because I didn't want to be an alcoholic. That was my rationale. But I drank after work every night. I would hit happy hour, two for the price of one, and have a couple of rounds there. I would go home and drink with my roommate if she happened to be home. If not, there was a nice glass of milk with Kahlúa in it before bed."

Cocaine and alcohol abuse did not seem to affect Cathy's performance on the job, and she was never reproached by her employer or questioned by a customer. Her addiction did wreak havoc on her finances, however, and she remains in debt to this day.

"I could have a hangover, do lines in the morning before I left for work, and be able to function. I very rarely called in sick. I'm very driven in that capacity," she says.

"But I maxed-out my credit cards. I jogged bills to afford coke. I wrote checks to the business so that I could get cash and then had to juggle finances to cover the check. I would call my dealer from the store, and he would deliver it to me right there at work. I bought coke so people would want to be with me.

"I lied and I stole from my employer for a long time and didn't think twice about it. I was never caught, and I've made amends for it today. I returned the money. They were shocked that I came forward, but I had to admit where I was wrong so I could move on. My credit cards were taken away, and to this day I don't have them back. I still owe $8,000 in past bills, and my credit is shot."

Eventually, snorting cocaine no longer got Cathy high and, although she never actually freebased or took any other kind of drug besides cocaine, she did start manufacturing what she refers to as "cocopuffs."

"I learned to smoke when I started doing cocaine, and I liked to smoke coke in my cigarettes. You take a knife or a pencil and pull out a bunch of the tobacco that's inside. You pat coke down in it, roll the end, and light it. We used to call them 'cocopuffs.' I would do that to a whole pack of cigarettes and sit in a restaurant and smoke them.

"It got me high quick. I never freebased, and I don't know what that high is like. But at the end of my addiction I couldn't get high just snorting it; I had to smoke it. I imagine it's similar and that I would eventually have learned to 'base if I had kept going."

Although burning coke "smells horrible," Cathy was only questioned once—by a co-worker after a party held for a new store opening. She denied that anything unusual had occurred, and the incident was never mentioned again.

While Cathy and Tami both considered alcohol their primary addiction, both are also certain that cocaine is what caused them to bottom out and, consequently, what led them to sobriety. "It speeded the end up," Tami concludes. "I'm grateful that I did cocaine because it speeded up my alcohol abuse too. Eventually, I would have ended up here. I was an alcoholic from the beginning, from the first time I ever drank, I think. It just would have taken a lot longer to convince me. My main addiction was alcohol, but cocaine put the icing on the cake."

Both women agree that, ironically, it was their mother who, though unaware of her children's addictions, ultimately led both of them to pursue sobriety. Anne was eight months sober and married for the fifth time, to a man who has been sober since 1970, when Tami sought help. Nineteen months later Cathy and her brother both joined them. Anne was shocked to discover that her children used cocaine.

"I never knew that it was hereditary until I went to A.A.," she says. "I thought they were normal teenagers. They were growing up. Drugs scared me; drinking didn't. I felt there was a big difference. It was so much denial on my part. I figured if I put my head in the sand, it would go away. I had no idea. I was crushed. I had high hopes for my kids."

"My mother never said anything to me, and I don't know that she was even aware that I had any kind of problem, but she was about eight months sober, and she had a glow, a sparkle in her eye. I can't describe it, but it was so beautiful," Tami reminisces.

Soon after that Tami had a hangover and again called in sick to her job as a secretary at an electronics company in Irvine. She then called her mother, who took her to an A.A. meeting the following day at lunch and again that evening.

"At that point I realized I would do just about anything to be a part of what my mom had found. So I introduced myself as an addict/ alcoholic, and I just started to bawl my eyes out. I cried through the entire meeting."

At times Cathy's description of her experiences—although they took place almost two years later—is eerily similar to her sister's, although they spoke about them on separate occasions.

"At Thanksgiving three years ago I was sitting around the table with my family, and they were all sober. My sister was in her first year. They had invited a bunch of people from A.A. over to the house. There was a glow in my mother's eyes that to this day I can't describe. At that point I realized they were all talking about sobriety. And although they were my family, I realized that I had nothing in common with these people, which was basically how I felt my entire life. So while they were talking about their lives and their newfound sobriety, I was running off to the car to do lines and get loaded.

"Then my younger brother got arrested the night of my natal birthday, which is four days before my sobriety birthday. He was 16 at the time and high on PCP. He threw a rock off an overpass on a freeway, and it smashed into the windshield of a car. I thought, 'Oh, my God, this is what's happened to my family.' There was a brief moment of clarity, and I got to see what my life was about. I wanted that gleam that was in my mother's eyes. I wanted that gleam that was in my sister's eyes. I didn't want to live the way that I was living.

"I don't even know how to describe it, but I had searched for so many things for so long to fix how I was feeling. All the chemicals, the food, the self-help books, the Cinderella complex. When somebody told me there was another way, that there were 12 Steps available to me, I took advantage of it, and I've stayed sober ever since.

"But my mother had no idea, not a clue. When I told her that I used cocaine, it broke her heart. She just couldn't believe that her little girl would do that."

Both Cathy and Tami are extremely thankful that they never reached the level of desperation that some addicts reach before going for help. "I didn't want to end up like my mother, and that's exactly what I did," Cathy laments. "It really blows my mind sometimes to think that I got caught up in something for so much of my life that's totally contradictory to everything I believe in. I look back now and wonder how I ever survived. I was a chameleon, and I wanted to be accepted and loved so badly that I was willing to do anything that it took.

"If I had been running around with the kind of people who committed robberies, there is no doubt in my mind that I would have done it too. I was very fortunate. I didn't prostitute myself, except emotionally. We were just out to have a good time.

"With addiction we do what it is we do in order to survive, and how we learn those survivial techniques is by trial and error. It's either learned from parents or learned from what we see. Sometimes it's just reaction, and it works. I functioned in a society that gave me the tools to function, which were alcohol and drugs. Thank God, some of us are fortunate enough to get an opportunity to live another life."

"I'm just real fortunate not to have gone to the lengths that some people have gone to," Tami concurs. "It's a real miracle that I'm here because other people had to do worse. But I really felt like I bottomed out spiritually and emotionally. I was constantly trying to find something to fix me. That's why I believe it's a disease of spiritual malady.

Because I'll tell you what I found in A.A. that same day: I found hope. I found a whole bunch of it, and it was absolutely beautiful."

But even today, Tami finds it hard to leave some of the lessons of her childhood behind, and it took a great deal of soul-searching to do this interview. "As an adult child of an alcoholic, I broke the rules," she exclaims. "I told secrets that my mom is going to know about. You're never supposed to say anything, and you especially shouldn't feel anything."

While Anne feels some guilt for her children's addictions, she's not sure she could have changed anything. Although she didn't grow up around her own father, she later learned that he had also been an alcoholic. And her daughters' father was an alcoholic who died at age 29 in a barroom brawl. Anne believes it's a hereditary disease.

Additionally, her own abuse and absence from her home certainly contributed to the problem and kept her from noting her children's erratic behavior. Perhaps, she admits, it is something that is just too painful to confront, even today.

"Looking back, I don't know how anything could have been prevented. I wasn't exposed to alcohol as a child; so I don't think that if I hadn't drunk, I could have averted my children from experimenting or going on to become addicted if the tendencies were there. I don't see how.

"There's a certain amount of guilt, but in order to maintain my sanity and to keep me from dwelling on the past, I had to get rid of it very quickly. I did that by working the fourth, fifth, and ninth steps of the program, which made me realize that everything was necessary to get us to where we are now."

Today Anne works as outreach coordinator for a large chemical-dependency-treatment program in southern California. In sobriety her relationships with all her children improve every day, although her daughters each realize there is still work to be done, repairs to be made.

"Right now, I'm in the best place I've ever been. All four of my kids are clean and sober, and I'm clean and sober, and I have positive input for the first time in my life."

Cathy, sober since 1986, works for an interior-design firm, and through her attendance of A.A. and Overeaters Anonymous meetings she is attempting to get her emotions in order.

"It's really nice that we can all look back on this stuff and laugh about it now," Cathy says. "Not that we're discounting it, but we understand so much more of it now.

"To honestly say that I will never drink again would be cutting myself short. But I have no desire today to drink or get loaded. The thought does come into my mind occasionally, but it just passes through. Drinking, using, and eating are not my problems. They were just symptoms of my disease. Living life is my problem. I just don't know how to cope with the daily things that most people just pass by. They're the end of the world for me.

"But I can change my life. My relationships today are a lot different than they used to be—with both men and women. I have women friends in my life who are really there for me, no matter what. They care about me as a person, not about how much drugs I have or if I'm going to pick up the bar tab. That's not what it's about today. It's about Cathy."

Today, Tami, married for seven years and sober since 1984, recently began working in employee recruitment and is very excited about the new career opportunity. She is the mother of a daughter, five, and a son, three, the latter born in sobriety. She sometimes mourns her lost childhood but doesn't dwell on it.

"Part of me really regrets that as a child I didn't have some of the things that the Brady kids had. I learned the values of the American family from those kinds of TV shows. But I believe I'm a really good mom today. I know being sober enables me to do that. If I was still drinking, I would probably be beating my kids.

"I won't say it gets better and better every day, because sometimes I take a step backwards. I have moments when I'm filled with fear and anxiety. I'm slowly learning how to communicate with my husband and how to become the mother I never had. I'm becoming the person that I used to get drunk and dream about."

SARAH

CRIMINAL DEFENSE LAWYER
WESTERN STATE

Sarah, now 32, was a recent law school graduate when her boyfriend, also a lawyer, introduced her to cocaine. It was an instantaneous love affair. Having grown up with two alcoholic parents, she was already a fairly heavy drinker, but her cocaine abuse escalated her drinking as well. Unable to function on the job or represent her clients adequately, Sarah knew she would eventually do enough damage to lose her license. Rather than be shamed in the legal community, she voluntarily quit practicing law. She was, she recalls vividly, quite concerned with her image. She then began part-time sales work and full-time drug and alcohol use. At the height of her addiction Sarah used at least a gram of cocaine and drank as much as a quart of hard liquor a day. Soon she was financially ruined and a complete recluse, self-exiled in an attempt to stay continuously high. With no funds and suffering severe withdrawals, she finally turned to a 12-Step program for help and later checked into a county detoxification program. She spent a year and a half in a halfway house. Today, sober since 1985, Sarah works as a public defender in a western state. She estimates that 80 to 90 percent of her clients have drug and/or alcohol problems. She gladly shares her own story with them.

Sarah was the oldest of four siblings raised in an alcoholically dysfunctional family. Her parents associated with other heavy drinkers, and no one seemed to notice that the kids were experimenting with alcohol themselves.

"I was 15 years old. My parents would party after church with a group of fairly big drinkers. Our church does not have tenets about not drinking. It's actually quite a social church. Most people associate strict and straight with church. I don't. I associate drinking with church and church with drinking. I think half the people my parents went to church with were alcoholics or at the very least heavy drinkers. Even the priest's wife was an alcoholic.

"We kids would sneak booze, get drunk, and throw up. I got deathly ill that first night. I don't think anyone noticed. All the parents were pretty much involved in their own drinking and socializing."

Sarah looks back on her first experience with alcohol as a pleasant one, but she did make a conscious decision at that time to pursue drinking until she found the high everyone else seemed to be enjoying. "A lot of alcoholics say they remember that great feeling they got the first time. I don't really have that euphoric memory of my first drink. But I know I decided that I must have done it wrong and that's why I got sick. So I just set out to drink different things and try not to get sick."

Sarah, who now attends meetings of Adult Children of Alcoholics (ACA) as well as other meetings for users, realizes that her childhood contributed greatly to the course of her life. Her younger brother is also a recovering addict, and one of her sisters is in ACA counseling.

"My father was in midlevel management, and my mother is a teacher. They are both practicing alcoholics to this day. My father tended to be a sloppy drunk. I've seen my father so drunk that he peed in the closet. My mother drank a lot but was much more functional. She did, however, have all the personality changes that go along with alcohol abuse.

"We weren't physically abused, but we were emotionally," Sarah recalls. "It was more the abuse of witness abuse, being a witness. We had to watch the craziness and the arguing and the fighting."

Although her mother was also an alcoholic, her ability to function "normally" allowed her to overlook her own problem. Sarah and her mother were both disgusted by her father's behavior but never did anything to change the situation. "My mother and I used to point fingers at my father and say, 'Oh what a disgusting alcoholic he is. We should divorce him, and one of these days we will.' But 'we' still haven't.

"At the time I didn't realize my mother was an alcoholic as well. I resented her a great deal for allowing us to remain in that situation, although I never actually told her so."

When Sarah took her first drink, she was a freshman in high school. It wasn't too long after that, that a date introduced her to her first illegal drug.

"I went out on a date and smoked some pot. I never really liked pot. It made me sleepy, out of control, and paranoid. But I was pretty open-minded to anything that would make me feel differently than I felt.

"I was in high school in the late sixties, early seventies. I tried acid a couple times, but I didn't do vast quantities. I mostly partied on the weekends and every now and then. But I associated partying with getting high. It was never social."

Sarah later decided to attend law school. Although she was entirely functional, she continued to drink "socially." In her second year she moved in with a fellow law student. An increasingly bad relationship with him eventually pushed her past socially acceptable boundaries of alcohol use.

"I drank a lot at night, partly because of family alcoholism and the emotional problems that came from that and partly because I was in a bad relationship. He was lying to me and cheating on me. I wasn't happy, and I didn't want to deal with reality; so I drank to hide my feelings. I would say to myself, 'No, I will not feel that. I *am* going to make this relationship work.' Then I would glug, glug, glug down some vodka or brandy."

Rather than leave her boyfriend, Sarah continued to drink more and more. After graduation they opened a law practice together. Within a year he had introduced her to cocaine as a sexual aid. She was 28 years old.

"What happened was I started passing out on him from drinking. He introduced me to cocaine to wake me up so we could have sex longer. That's how it started. I got hooked right away. I had a very short period of euphoria. But once I started, I could not stop.

"Number one, it sobered me up so that I could think clearly, or so I thought, and I could drink more. I also felt like I had a vivacious personality and could talk. And I guess in the beginning I felt real sexual. But quite frankly it quickly had a reverse effect. I liked cocaine, and I think sex was the price I paid—I lost interest in it. Cocaine really didn't serve its purpose other than to keep me awake. But I didn't let on, because I wanted more coke."

Sarah very quickly got caught up in the vicious cycle of addiction, wanting to attain that initial high again and never having quite enough cocaine to sustain it.

"It was a real exhilarating high. But it only lasts a short while, and then it starts to drop off. You keep trying to get back to that high, and you never quite make it."

Sarah describes, almost lovingly, how the act of doing cocaine became more of a sexual stimulant to her than the actual sex. "The ritual of laying out a line became a real fascination and a real high in itself. That was part of what we did—drank, did cocaine, and had sex. They went together. The feeling is hard to describe. It's like when you're really hungry for something sweet, and you see a hot-fudge sundae.

"You're just imagining what it will be like, experiencing some of the thrill before doing it. You're laying out a line and watching how big it's going to be, especially if someone else is doing it. It's the anticipation of that initial charge. The euphoria itself is very short-lived, but the intensity is so great and the draw is so great that you keep doing it."

Eventually, more than five years after it began, Sarah found the courage to leave such a severely dysfunctional relationship when she met another lawyer, to whom she was attracted, at a golf tournament. They moved in together.

Although she was now living with the other man, for six months she continued to practice law with her ex-boyfriend and go home to her new boyfriend at night. She finally broke the tie completely and began to practice in the offices of her new beau, also a heavy cocaine and alcohol abuser.

"Shortly after I started using drugs with my first boyfriend, the relationship broke up. I hooked up with another lawyer who was a regular cocaine user. But I dragged the other relationship out for six months. It was horrible."

Today Sarah realizes she has a male dependency problem, which, most experts agree, is a common trait among women raised in dysfunctional families and/or who have addiction problems. "I was absolutely dependent on the men in my life. I turned over all decisions to them. They controlled my salary because I worked for them. And I would just generally adopt their preferences—whether it was food, drink, or TV programming. Whatever they wanted was what I wanted. That's a frequent problem among women who grew up in chemically dependent families, and it's a self-esteem issue that often co-exists with addiction. They're hard to separate."

It didn't take long for Sarah and her new live-in to establish a pattern of constant drinking and using. Soon, perhaps influenced by the substance abuse, she found her mate to be abusive.

"In my new relationship we got into regular cocaine use almost immediately. We would drink and do cocaine and drink and do cocaine. He would buy eight balls, which are an eighth of a ounce of coke, and we would suck it all up.

"He turned out to be not only a cocaine addict, but a severe alcoholic as well. Halfway through his third drink I would watch him turn into a crazy man straight out of *Dr. Jekyll and Mr. Hyde*. This was a nightly thing, his screaming and yelling and calling me a whore and everything else under the sun. He was always yelling at me for something, and he would spit in my face and push me around. It was insanity—to the point where he would chase me around the house and I would hide in a closet and pile clothes on top of myself. I would huddle in the dark, trembling for fear he would find me.

"He didn't actually hit me. That was the boundary. I said that if he ever hit me, I was going to leave. Would I have left if he actually had hit me? I don't know. I was so emotionally drained yet so dependent on him, both financially and for drugs, there's a good chance I would have made an excuse and said, 'Well, he didn't mean it. He was high, and he's going through withdrawals. That's all it is.' "

Although the boyfriend Sarah was now living and practicing law with was another addict, she hid the severity of her using from him. "I was using his drugs, but I also started buying my own so I didn't have to ask for it. I had two dealers going on the side so neither man would know how much I was using. I didn't want my boyfriend or anyone else to know how out of control I was.

"Within a year I was using at least a gram a day; but I never spent any more than $100 a day. I set that boundary for myself. If I ran out, if I did all of my $100 worth of cocaine, that was it for the day. I just shook until I came down. I suppose I thought that meant I had control. I never even thought of the word *addict*. I didn't know what that word meant, and I had no concept of 'I can't stop.'

"My excuse would be, 'I stayed up too late last night, and I need a pick-me-up today.' Or 'I have to stay late and finish this research and the coke helps me to stay up.' Then it was, 'Well, I had a glass of wine at lunch, so I need a line to wake me up.'

It was during this time that Sarah, afraid her boyfriend would discover the depth of her addiction, allowed herself to be placed in very dangerous situations on a number of occasions. "He owned an airplane and was sort of teaching me to fly. He would give me the controls and let me steer the plane, even take it off the ground. So we'd fly places, and he'd ask me to take the controls.

"When he knew we were flying, he wouldn't do anything the entire day beforehand, drink or use drugs. He had that much control at times. But I took that airplane off while I was high on cocaine. If I had refused, he would have known I was doing drugs, and I didn't want him to find out.

"That was incredibly scary, just terrifying. I was so out of control. Then I would say something like, 'Oh, I feel dizzy because I haven't eaten. You take over.' I'd find a way to do it without having to admit I was high."

Sarah regarded her "flying lessons" as one of the marks of her social prestige. Very image-conscious and always groomed immaculately, no matter to what depths her addiction took her, she also factored into this image her use of cocaine and her indulgence in quality liquors.

"I was always very image-conscious—that's why the cocaine, the airplane, the name-brand booze, all those things. I drank only name-brand liquors, mostly vodka and brandy. But to switch off, I would try tricky things, like drinking crème de menthe. I was afraid I smelled like booze and hoped to smell like mint.

"I was the young, successful yuppie. I felt like part of the in-crowd. I thought, 'Cool people do this, the people who have made it.' Except that in the back of my mind I knew that I was doing too much. But I didn't realize that until I had been using for a year."

It was not only Sarah's personal life that was out of control. She was also falling apart on the job and was now unable to represent her clients adequately. "I was working out of my boyfriend's office. I had hardly any clients of my own. I couldn't return their phone calls, I wasn't doing their work, and I was missing deadlines. I'd have a canned martini in my drawer and a line laid out on that little table shelf that pulls out of a desk. I'd do my own coke and then do some in my boyfriend's office."

Though Sarah did not spend much time in court at this point in her career, she does recall one incident that makes her pale today. Although she was terrified her addiction would be discovered within the law community, her cocaine use was becoming increasingly compulsive, and she was taking bigger risks, tempting fate.

"We didn't do drugs around people who wouldn't approve, but we did some really risky things. We did coke in the corridor of the federal courthouse. We'd go down the hall and look around furtively and then each do a couple of spoons. Then we'd go back to court.

"There were other lawyers and guards and judges all over the place. God, they would have loved that, two lawyers doing cocaine in the federal courthouse." She can't quite recollect what kind of case they were representing, only that it was her boyfriend who actually presented the argument. A highly emotional person without drugs, his speech became melodramatic while under the influence of cocaine.

"He was an intense person anyway; so the coke just intensified all of that. He would get real emotional, real dramatic. He was the kind of attorney who can cry giving a closing argument, he'd get that involved."

Although avoiding physical withdrawal was the primary reason they chose to snort coke in compromising situations, the exhilarating naughtiness of it all was also a contributing factor for Sarah. "There was definitely that side to it, an edge of danger or excitement, an awareness of, 'Oh, my God, we're in the federal courthouse.' But it was more that if you started doing cocaine in the morning, you couldn't stop. You wanted to continue throughout the day; so you took some with you."

Sarah feels that it's "pretty human" for lawyers and judges to be able to overlook the law they've sworn to uphold. She just never let herself think about it, thereby avoiding the conflict. "I never really considered it, never really looked at it. It wasn't even that I thought about it and said, 'Oh, well, who cares?' It was more like putting on blinders than anything else.

"I know it's a completely different situation from cocaine use, but I see lawyers today driving 75 miles an hour down the freeway who wouldn't think twice about taking someone else to court for breaking that same speeding law."

Sarah also attributes some of the extreme work pressure and unhappiness within the law community with her need to escape from reality. While the American Bar Association has no figures on the extent of the problem, many experts agree that substance abuse affects at least 15 percent of all lawyers and judges, and some venture it may go as high as 30 percent. In the general population the estimate is 10 to 12 percent.

"There's a lot of pressure and responsibility in law. You're dealing with other people, and your job is to take care of their problems. You still have your own problems too. And somehow, in legal situations neither side is really happy. Usually the law and judges work out some sort of compromise, and no one wants to compromise; we all want to win. With so much unhappiness and pressure and considering the deadlines and threats of malpractice, it's really nice to just settle down and make it all go away—just for a while."

Sarah's chosen profession didn't consciously keep her from resorting to stealing or dealing to support her habit, but she's convinced that it was a subconscious deterrent. "I was terrified of getting caught. Knowing that I was a lawyer, I anticipated that if I got caught, it would be news. I was terrified of the exposure and public humiliation, not to mention going to jail. That was part of why I eventually left the law."

But no one ever confronted Sarah about her use. Eventually, health problems and an increasing difficulty with performing everyday tasks prompted her to give up her profession.

"The cocaine and drinking went together; so I'm not real clear on what caused what. But by the end I constantly had bleeding gums, I started to get those little veins on my nose, my back and shoulders were broken out from being in sweats from withdrawals, and I was pretty severely malnourished. Somewhere in my mind I knew that not eating anything was real unhealthy, and I would force myself to gag down a tortilla with cheese. But sometimes that was all I would eat for a couple weeks at a time. I ate just enough to subsist on.

"I don't remember hearing about specific mistakes I made, but that doesn't mean they didn't tell me. I did hear later that one client had gone back to my old boyfriend and said, 'She's not okay; there's something wrong.' But nobody said anything to me.

"I was missing deadlines or meeting them right up against the wire. Everything was an absolute emergency, and secretaries had to stay late to do the typing because I was too high to get the work done earlier."

There was one specific incident, in which she "dropped the ball" on a friend's divorce case, that actually pushed her out the door. "What finally made me leave the law practice was a friend of mine. I had started her divorce and done a marital-property-settlement agreement when they reconciled. Then she called me back and said, 'Forget it. He's screwing up again, I want to go through with the divorce.' I said, 'Yeah, right. Okay.' But I couldn't do it, because I couldn't stay sober long enough.

"She kept calling, and I kept dodging her phone calls and making excuses. Then I had a secretary dodging her phone calls and making excuses. Finally, I just dropped out. I left her a message saying, 'I'm sorry, but I can't handle this right now. I have a personal problem.'

"Not that anything necessarily changed right away. Messing up my friend's divorce was devastating to me, but I was addicted and couldn't stop. I was very aware that this was getting out of hand and I had a problem. I was very ashamed of myself and particularly remorseful because it was my friend. I still haven't found her to make my amends for that. I haven't seen her since 1984."

Sarah also left the law practice because she found it was no longer possible to camouflage the extent of her use from her partner/boyfriend. Additionally, she explains, she moved out of his house in a feeble attempt to quit using altogether.

"There was no way for me to hide it anymore. So I snuck away in the middle of the night. I took a few clothes and pushed my car out of the driveway. I thought that once I was away from the stress of this abusive relationship, my drinking and cocaine use would be social. And that just didn't happen."

Although Sarah lived with two separate men over a period of seven years, she had never stopped making payments on her own house, and that's where she now took refuge. She stayed cooped up for a month and then made a decision to begin selling Tupperware to support herself. An old high school friend interceded, however, and offered her a job as a sales representative in the electronics industry.

"I was going to sell Tupperware at night. That way, I figured, I wouldn't start drinking and using, at least until I came home from my Tupperware party. Also, I wouldn't have to get up in the morning. But I ran into an old friend who said, 'Come work for me if you want to do sales.'

"I did that for about a year. I had one decent-sized sale, but for the most part I put on my answering machine, stayed home, did coke, and drank. Since it was a manufacturer's rep job, there were district sales reps under me, and I got commissions on other people's sales. Just enough was happening so that it wasn't clear I wasn't doing anything myself.

"One gaffe does stand out in my mind, however. It was on a business trip to Arizona. I had been doing coke and drinking before I went on this sales call with some of the top engineers of an electronics firm. I couldn't show them my stuff, because I was shaking so badly. I was trembling from head to toe and couldn't hold my hands still. I think they thought I was nervous. I don't know if anyone knew what was going on."

In a year's time Sarah had become a total recluse, locked in the house, rarely leaving, even for work. The house was a mess, and her mail was piling up at the door. "By that time fear and paranoia had started to settle in on me, and I had pretty much locked myself in the house. I was afraid of everything and everybody. Here I was, alone, without either man—I always thought they were 'forcing' me to use—and I was still using. I couldn't stop.

"My mail was piling up. I had big bundles, three inches thick and rubberbanded together. They were all late notices that I couldn't deal with. My house was a mess, although I wasn't dirtying any dishes, because I ate almost nothing.

"I never attempted suicide, although it used to cross my mind. I would just sit there and rock and cry and cry. I'd beat myself on the chest, trying to make it hurt on the outside instead of the inside. The depression, the paranoia, and the pain were so great. Suicide actually crossed my mind more vividly after I got clean because then I had nothing to kill the pain anymore except hours of therapy, and that can be painful too."

Eventually, out of cash and deeply in debt, Sarah stopped using cocaine, but she continued to drink heavily. "I wasn't making a lot of money," she explains, "but I used to have great credit. I had several credit cards with $1,000 to $4,000 limits. I was taking out cash advances to pay for cocaine, and when they ran out, that's when I stopped. There was nowhere for the money to come from.

"Also, even worse, were the withdrawals. They became so horrible. I couldn't stay high all the time, and I couldn't stand coming down anymore. It was so painful. I thought my heart was going to explode, and I felt like I was coming unglued, like I was going to shatter into a million, billion pieces. It was so excruciating, and I shook so badly. I just decided never to do it again.

"But I wasn't quite ready to surrender yet. I drank for another six to eight months. I thought I was drinking to come down off cocaine, and that if I stopped doing coke, I would drink less. But it worked the other way around. My body's tolerance and requirement for alcohol had increased; so when I quit doing cocaine, I couldn't stop drinking. I was drinking a quart of hard liquor a day.

"And now, without the cocaine, I couldn't stay awake and function either; so I would just drink and pass out, drink and pass out around the clock. Then I'd sober up for a day and get a few things done, make a few phone calls, make one or two sales calls a week, but be home by four or five o'clock and drink until midnight. Some days I wouldn't make it out for my sales calls. I would cancel them, make excuses, not even reschedule appointments."

Afraid of what people might think until the bitter end, Sarah kept up all pretenses of normality. Still, no one suspected, or at least no one said anything to her.

"I was just alone, drinking. But every now and then I would get myself together and go out and do something social. I'd control my drinking while I was out. They'd say, 'Let's go home and do this,' or 'Let's go out and do that.' I'd say, 'Gee, I would if I could, but I have to work tomorrow; so I better go home,' knowing full well that what I was going to do was go home and drink myself into oblivion.

"But right to the end, even when I was drinking around the clock, I would get up in the morning, take a glass of vodka into the shower with me, blow-dry my hair, put on eye makeup, get dressed, and then go back to bed and drink. I never looked like I was falling apart.

Behind closed doors I could tell, but in the outside world, nobody knew."

No longer subject to cocaine withdrawals, Sarah did continue to suffer debilitating hangovers.

"Oh, my God, they were just incredible, horrendous—the shaking and nausea. That was sometimes part of why I drank in the morning. You've heard of 'hair of the dog that bit you?' That means, take a drink to raise your alcohol level back up and get rid of the symptoms of withdrawal. That's what a hangover is: withdrawal. It's your body detoxing itself from overindulgence.

"I used to wake up and look at myself in the mirror and say, 'My God, I did it again. I don't believe that I did it again. I'm never going to do this again.' And that night I would do it again. Day after day after day. Finally I saw it. I said, 'Oh, I see. I can't stop.' "

One day Sarah was telling a friend at work a tale of "poor me," though skipping over the part about her using. He surprised Sarah by inquiring if she had grown up in an alcoholic family. She admitted she had, and he gave her some literature on Adult Children of Alcoholics. At age 32 it was a turning point.

"I started going to meetings. It was there that I saw a woman who looked like myself, who was educated and dressed businesslike, and who admitted to her addiction. She said the magic words, 'I *could not* control my drinking and drug use.'

"I went on one last bender after that, and I called for help the next day. I called Alcoholics Anonymous, and I went to every meeting they offered all day long, three to four meetings a day, for a very long time.

"I went through some serious withdrawals that continued for quite a while. I remember the cocaine withdrawals as being more intense, but the alcohol withdrawals went on longer. The trembling and shaking went on for weeks, but for 90 days I had really horrible pains in my joints. Nobody was ever able to diagnose it, but it was just excruciating, and nothing helped.

"Even after the physical trembling stopped, inside I felt that I was rattling apart. And the depression was overwhelming. It was all I could do to get myself up in the morning, take a shower, and go down to A.A. I was real afraid of using again. In essence, I think I had an emotional breakdown. I couldn't function.

"I had thought that once I cleaned up for two weeks, I would be able to work triple time, catch up on all my work, and get back on track. But as each week went by, I was worse instead of better. I couldn't think straight. I couldn't connect one thought to another."

With no insurance and no cash to check into a privately run program that would be more intense than A.A., Sarah ended up spending seven days in a county detoxification program funded by the government. She was appalled.

"I was horrified," she laughs today. "There were some people who were basically street people, but they were shaking and depressed and craving drugs and alcohol just like me. I was so broken by that time, and I was so desperate for some sort of help that my mind opened up to the humanity in everybody.

"There was a businessman there who had lost it all, some street people, some young people, some older people, some blue-collar workers. It didn't take that long to see that I was the same as everyone else."

Sarah admits today that her initial haughtiness interfered with her recovery process when she first entered treatment. "Because I tended to intellectualize so much, it was almost a hindrance to my recovery. To keep myself different, I took a book bag with me. I was going to take the scientific approach. I had books on recovery, the A.A. book, and pamphlets from all the 12-Step programs. I had a journal to write in, and my plan was to take good notes, which I did, and learn recovery faster than everyone else because I was so smart and so educated. That was how I approached it, like a class.

"But I was so intellectual that it made it difficult to be honest with myself. And a whole lot of recovery is what we call rigorous honesty. It's about everything that's going on inside you: to thine own self be true, know thyself, and all those kinds of things. Those are concepts that you deal with constantly in recovery and 12-Step programs."

After detoxing, Sarah decided to give up the lease on her home and move into a state-run halfway house, where recovering addicts live under supervision but in a homelike setting. Sarah's stay was considerably longer than is customary for residents. She spent 1½ years there, during which time she continued to attend one or two A.A. meetings a day in addition to private therapy.

It was nine months before Sarah attempted any kind of work—it took her that long to attend to her immediate physical and emotional problems. When she finally did take a job, it was an occasional stint for minimum wage, stuffing envelopes for the National Council on Alcoholism.

"I had a lot of dental work done because I almost ruined some of my teeth with the drugs, drinking, and malnutrition. And my liver was swollen. But, you know, my doctor had never noticed anything. Once I even donated blood while I was doing cocaine, and they said, 'Whoa, your blood pressure's up.' I said, 'Yeah, I've been working hard.' "

Eventually, Sarah took on a slightly more taxing position as a receptionist/secretary; however, she had done so much damage to her brain that she continued to find it difficult to function. "I had fried my brains so badly that I could barely look at the words and turn around and remember them long enough to type. I'd say it took two or two and a half years before I felt like I was getting back any mental stamina."

Sarah later decided to go back to school to become a veterinarian. She did part-time bookkeeping to help pay her rent and tuition. Shame kept her from returning to law.

"At this point, I didn't think I would go back into law. I was so ashamed of myself and so full of the fear of failure. I had never screwed up my license. That's one of the reasons I backed out. I knew I was in trouble, and I figured I'd better get out quick. But I didn't ever want to show my face in the legal community again. Although hardly anybody knew, I was afraid they would find out.

"I love animals, and animals love you, no matter what. But then I thought of all those years of science classes, and knew I wasn't going to make it as a vet. I love animals, but I didn't want to be treating other people's pets' worms. Plus, I was going to be 41 by the time I got out of school."

She was afraid to go back to the law because as a well-educated woman and a lawyer, Sarah felt she should have known better. A knowledgeable friend in A.A. forced her to overcome her fear.

"I had an A.A. sponsor who knew the depth of my shame. One of the reasons I didn't get help for so long was because I was so ashamed of myself. I thought, 'Oh, my God, look at what I've become. I'm going to have to do something about this tomorrow.'

"I think ego keeps people from obtaining help. Lawyers are supposed to be so darn self-sufficient, educated, intelligent, and, God knows, they're supposed to obey the law. They don't want to tell any-body, because they're too ashamed and afraid.

"Yet in recovery my sponsor made me tell everybody to get past that shame. By being forced to do that, I found that the stigma I was afraid would be there truly isn't. Almost without exception I have never had anybody react with anything other than, 'Well, good for you. Congratulations.'

"There are several judges and lawyers in my A.A. meetings. There's also a group called The Other Bar, for chemically dependent lawyers. It's a self-help group to bridge the gap between being afraid to ask for help and the 12-Step programs."

It was at A.A. that Sarah met another lawyer who gave her a little push back into the practice of law. A series of events eventually helped her land her lcurrent job as a public defender.

"About the time I decided that changing careers wasn't really what I wanted to do, I met a lawyer in A.A. I told him, 'I *might* be inter-ested in getting back into law. But why don't I come to court and watch what you do?' He said, 'You don't need to come watch me. I just need these cases continued—*boomp,* here, you go do it.'

"Then there was just a whole series of coincidences, but in A.A. we say there are no accidents. Doors started opening; miracles started happening. I bumped into people who referred me to people who set me up here and there. I ended up doing some volunteer work at one of the arraignment courts, eventually got hired on as a contractor and then as an employee for the defender's office." Today, having been back in law for 2½ years, Sarah feels that her experiences have added a whole other dimension to her practice.

"Not long ago a judge who's a friend of mine in A.A. made a com-ment to me. He said, 'You want my advice, switch sides.' Meaning, go over to the prosecutor's office because it's more prestigious. If you want something on your résumé, it's better to be a district attorney than a public defender. Because people make comments to me like, 'Public defender. Does that mean you represent slimebags?' And I say, 'No, it means I make sure that people's constitutional rights are pro-tected so that they're treated fairly.'

"I said, 'You know, Judge, I couldn't do that. I've done too many drugs. It would be bad karma for me to go to the prosecutor's office and try to put people in jail for what I did.' I'm real open. Judges and pretty much everyone else I work with know that I'm recovering.

"In the public defender's office I would say that 80 to 90 percent of the people I see have drug and alcohol problems. I feel my experience gives me more than compassion, it gives me empathy. I know what they're going through. I also have vast resources for recovery that I'm familiar with on a personal basis. I'm not going to refer them to a $15,000 hospital program."

Although she was forced to declare a $15,000 bankruptcy and only recently started dating again, at 36 years of age Sarah's life today is well on its way to being—if it isn't already—wonderful.

"I ruined my finances, but it wasn't huge. I have an attorney friend who was addicted to cocaine and declared an $80,000 bankruptcy. I still have issues that I'm working on, but I'm not in any kind of pain like I was before.

"But my life today is so incredible compared to what it had become. I hit a pretty low bottom. What we talk about in the program is keeping that memory green.

"I never want to go back to that place. I never want to be hitting myself to make it hurt on the outside instead of the inside. I never want to go through drug withdrawals, feeling like my heart and my brain are going to explode any minute, shaking from head to toe, sweating profusely, and feeling like I'm going to blow apart into a million pieces.

"I really doubt that I could live through those kinds of things again, now that I've recovered and felt happiness and peace and serenity. But even today," she laments, "if I see lines of coke laid out in a movie or an ad, I still remember the intensity of that feeling and the draw. It was like a magnet. My recovery is strong enough that I don't want to do it, but I still feel it."

DIFFICULT QUESTIONS:

AM I AN ADDICT, AND TO WHOM DO I TURN?

Anonymous groups recognize that all addicts "bottom out" before seeking help, but that bottom is however an addict perceives it. It may not be earth-shattering, and it may not be the loss of job, marriage, or standing within the community—items that allow many addicts to rationalize their behavior. Perhaps it's the development of a health problem, debilitating hangovers, under-the-influence actions that are contrary to your values, or just an overriding knowledge that you're no longer in control and that the problem can only progress and get worse.

Are you an addict? This is something only you can answer. The following questionnaire,* compiled by members of Narcotics Anonymous, will provide guidelines for you to judge whether or not you have an addiction problem.

1. Do you ever use alone?
2. Have you ever substituted one drug for another, thinking that one particular drug was the problem?
3. Have you ever manipulated or lied to a doctor to obtain prescription drugs?
4. Have you ever stolen drugs or stolen to obtain drugs?

*Am I an Addict? Reprinted with permission from Narcotics Anonymous World Service Office, Inc., Van Nuys, Calif.

5. Do you regularly use a drug when you wake up or when you go to bed?
6. Have you ever taken one drug to overcome the effects of another?
7. Do you avoid people or places that do not approve of your using drugs?
8. Have you ever used a drug without knowing what it was or what it would do to you?
9. Has your job or school performance ever suffered from the effects of your drug use?
10. Have you ever been arrested as a result of using drugs?
11. Have you ever lied about what or how much you use?
12. Do you put the purchase of drugs ahead of your financial responsibilities?
13. Have you ever tried to stop or control your using?
14. Have you ever been in a jail, hospital, or drug-rehabilitation center because of your using?
15. Does using interfere with your sleeping or eating?
16. Does the thought of running out of drugs terrify you?
17. Do you feel it is impossible for you to live without drugs?
18. Do you ever question your own sanity?
19. Is your drug use making life at home unhappy?
20. Have you ever thought you couldn't fit in or have a good time without drugs?
21. Have you ever felt defensive, guilty, or ashamed about using?
22. Do you think a lot about drugs?
23. Have you had irrational or indefinable fears?
24. Has using affected your sexual relationships?
25. Have you ever taken drugs you didn't prefer?
26. Have you ever used drugs because of emotional pain or stress?
27. Have you ever overdosed on any drugs?
28. Do you continue to use despite negative consequences?
29. Do you think you might have a drug problem?

There is no set number of affirmative answers that indicate you are addicted; however, many recovering addicts and experts feel that if you're questioning your own behavior, if you've gone far enough to pick up this book, take this test, or seek other help or advice, you have already admitted, at least to yourself, that you are out of control.

Once you've made that admission, overcoming the "Donna Reed syndrome" and asking for help is a difficult proposition for even today's most modern, independent woman. But there is help available to anyone who truly desires it.

12-STEP PROGRAMS: POWER TO THE PEOPLE

Only one route to recovery has been structured to make it available to everyone, regardless of gender, age, race, financial resources, and religion or lack of religion. Further, a woman does not have to leave her home, interrupt her day-to-day activities, or endanger her position within the community by revealing her full identity. There's no fee, and groups meet frequently almost everywhere in the continental United States, or if a woman lives in a remote area, a group can be started as long as there are two or more people willing to become members.

A woman who has an addiction problem can join a local chapter of an anonymous, 12-Step program, where she will find both understanding and support on her road to sobriety.

Cocaine Anonymous (C.A.), founded in 1982, lists more than 1,200 groups in the U.S. and Canada and is the country's fastest-growing fellowship.

Narcotics Anonymous (N.A.), founded in 1953, now lists more than 14,000 groups and gives an additional 3,000 introductory presentations to the residents of hospitals and institutions. N.A. groups exist across the U.S., in many parts of Canada, and in 43 foreign countries.

Alcoholics Anonymous (A.A.), founded in 1935, is the oldest and most broad-based of the groups. A.A. now lists well over 76,000 groups worldwide, almost 40,000 of them located in the U.S. Overseas, there are memberships in 118 countries.

Women for Sobriety (WFS), established in 1975, is a fledgling feminist group of approximately 300 U.S. meetings, also anonymous, that follows 13 statements oriented toward the specific needs of women.

Overeaters Anonymous (O.A.) may also be a useful reference for a woman whose chemical dependency is linked to an eating disorder. Founded in 1960, O.A. also follows a 12-Step program and lists 9,000 groups worldwide, of which 8,000 are established in the U.S. and Canada.

These groups, which are not formally associated, hold daily meetings that are open to anyone who is battling an addiction and who needs help and fellowship to achieve sobriety. It is strongly suggested that a woman whose primary addiction is cocaine attend C.A. or N.A., rather than A.A.

What Should I Expect?

A woman walking into an anonymous meeting for the first time should expect to meet other addicts, male and female, who identify themselves only by their first names. For many professional people such as doctors, nurses, lawyers, judges, schoolteachers, pilots, police officers, and so on, it is crucial to their careers to maintain their anonymity. For others it is simply a personal desire. Depending on how densely populated your hometown is, the meeting could be extremely small or, in an urban area, as large as 30 to 40.

A newcomer will encounter others who have a personal understanding of what she is experiencing. They know you are apprehensive and frightened. Most groups offer refreshments either prior to or immediately following the meeting, providing a social environment for a newcomer to meet other recovering addicts. The therapeutic value of one addict helping another is without parallel, and it is suggested that new members take down numbers of people they speak with and use them freely, day or night.

Most meetings follow a more or less set pattern, although distinctive variations have developed in some areas. There are no group leaders at anonymous meetings, but revolving elected "officials" will call the meeting to order and briefly describe the program for the benefit of newcomers.

Members, in an open-forum setting, voluntarily and briefly share their experiences, strengths, and hope for an hour to an hour and a half. During the meeting the group observes and celebrates the anniversary of any member's sobriety, beginning with 30 days. The honoree may receive a cake and is presented with a key chain–like "chip" that commemorates the occasion. Though of no financial value, a chip is a badge of honor and much treasured. Since anonymous groups are associated with no outside organization and accept no outside financing, a basket will be passed for voluntary contributions to defray the costs of the meeting.

Anonymous programs support complete abstinence from all drugs, including alcohol, no matter what you consider your primary addiction to be. An addictive personality will most likely be susceptible to any mind-altering substance.

It is suggested that all newcomers attempting to achieve sobriety initially attend at least 90 meetings in 90 days to help establish a pattern of not using and to control the compulsion and obsession to use that may be overwhelming at first. You should develop an external focus, jump in, and become a part of the group. You may want to volunteer to set up chairs, make coffee, or assist in other ways.

Also, as soon as you find someone with whom you feel comfortable enough to confide in and who has celebrated at least one year of sobriety, you may request her to be your "sponsor." This person, who should be a member of the same sex, will serve as a confidant, will talk you through difficult times when you may be tempted to use, and will offer you the benefit of her own achievement of sobriety on a one-to-one basis of communication.

It is also recommended by C.A. that newcomers read the group's literature and regularly read and refer to the 575-page book, *Alcoholics Anonymous*, more commonly referred to as the "Big Book" by members. N.A. has its own version of this publication, *Narcotics Anonymous*, frequently called the "Basic Text."

Originally written in 1939 by A.A. founder Bill W., the Big Book has been updated twice (1955, 1976) but retains unchanged its coverage of the principles that led its earliest members to sobriety, along with a representative cross section of members' personal stories. In this book you will find the crux of the membership's crusade for sobriety.

What If I Fail?

No one becomes addicted in a day, and anonymous programs suggest you treat yourself gently and take your efforts to achieve sobriety just one day at a time. Even one day of sobriety, they say, is a miracle. Don't overwhelm yourself by looking too far ahead. Consider this day only. If you fall down today, ask for additional support and consider the next day.

The program is not based on religion, but on a spiritual well-being. The program encourages a newcomer to form her own interpretation of a higher being. It is also based on the belief that addiction is not a moral shortcoming, but an uncontrollable disease. Members of an anonymous program are not interested in your past, only in what you want to do about your problem today.

The 12 Steps Revisited

All of these recovery programs work on the premise that each member accepts the group's philosophy and agrees to personally "work" or practice, each and every day, 12 "Steps" to achieving lasting sobriety. Though it's likely that most adults have at least heard of the anonymous programs, they may not be familiar with the exact nature of the group's philosophy.

The 12 Steps of Cocaine Anonymous are as follows:

1. We admitted that we were powerless over cocaine and all other mind-altering substances—that our lives had become unmanageable.
2. Came to believe that a Power greater than ourselves could restore us to sanity.
3. Made a decision to turn our will and our lives over to the care of God *as we understood Him.*
4. Made a searching and fearless moral inventory of ourselves.
5. Admitted to God, to ourselves, and to another human being the exact nature of our wrongs.
6. Were entirely ready to have God remove all these defects of character.
7. Humbly asked Him to remove our shortcomings.
8. Made a list of all persons we had harmed and became willing to make amends to them all.
9. Made direct amends to such people whenever possible, except when to do so would injure them or others.
10. Continued to take personal inventory, and when we were wrong, promptly admitted it.
11. Sought through prayer and meditation to improve our conscious contact with God *as we understood Him,* praying only for knowledge of His will for us and the power to carry that out.
12. Having had a spiritual awakening as the result of these steps, we tried to carry this message to addicts and to practice these principles in all our affairs.

Why You Can Trust These Groups

Additionally, there are 12 Traditions of anonymous groups that are, without exception, observed for the common good of everyone in the organization. As with the Steps, C.A.'s Traditions were adapted from the Traditions of A.A., which came into being in the fellowship's first decade as it began to grow substantially. Written in 1946 and formally adopted in 1950, they are meant to preserve the group's attitudes, spiritual principles, and informal structure.

The 12 Traditions of Cocaine Anonymous are as follows:

1. Our common welfare should come first; personal recovery depends upon C.A. unity.
2. For our group purpose there is but one ultimate authority—a loving God as He may express Himself in our group conscience. Our leaders are but trusted servants; they do not govern.
3. The only requirement for membership is a desire to stop using.
4. Each group should be autonomous except in matters affecting other groups or C.A. as a whole.
5. Each group has but one primary purpose—to carry the message to the addict who still suffers.
6. A C.A. group ought never endorse, finance, or lend the C.A. name to any related facility or outside enterprise, lest problems of money, property, and prestige divert us from our primary purpose.
7. Every C.A. group ought to be fully self-supporting, declining outside contributions.
8. C.A. should remain forever nonprofessional, but our service centers may employ special workers.
9. C.A. as such ought never be organized, but we may create service boards or committees directly responsible to those they serve.
10. C.A. has no opinion on outside issues; hence the C.A. name ought never be drawn into public controversy.
11. Our public relations policy is based on attraction rather than promotion; we need always maintain personal anonymity at the level of press, radio, and films.
12. Anonymity is the spiritual foundation of all our traditions, ever reminding us to place principles before personalities.

The 12 Steps and 12 Traditions are reprinted and adapted with permission of Alcoholics Anonymous World Services, Inc. Please see original A.A. versions on pages 195–198.

Making a Lifetime Commitment

Achieving sobriety is not just a matter of physically attending meetings and reading literature, it's making a lifelong commitment to living an entirely different lifestyle—physically and emotionally—without the "benefit" of mind-altering or emotion-numbing substances. It demands that you embrace the 12 Steps and Traditions and learn how to live life on life's terms. It won't be easy by any means, but it will be one of the most rewarding efforts of your entire life, as C.A. members testify:

"To say I'm a fan is a very mild word for my feelings about the 12-Step program. It saved my life," enthuses one attendee, sober since 1982. "Nobody wants to be rigorously honest, admit her faults to others, or live with these kinds of principles in her life unless she's going to die without it. I was just so beat up by this disease that there was no other way to go except to be humble, do it their way, and do what I needed to do to survive. As soon as you feel you can handle it your way one more time, that's when you use again.

"I'm not saying there are no other paths to the goal of sobriety, but this is the best, most tried-and-true way for people who are addicted to achieve long-term recovery and to be comfortable in their own skins. As someone whose life has been transformed by it, I believe in it with all my heart and soul. It works for me and a lot of other people."

"There are still the problems and the ups and downs," adds one other member, sober since 1983, "but at least I now have the tools to get through them without using, and it's wonderful."

I HURT *THEM* THE MOST

Most of the time it is not only the addict's life that has been severely affected by her addiction. She may have done emotional damage to her parents, husband, children, friends, co-workers, or others. And in sobriety she will be forced to address her actions while using. The eighth and ninth Steps of the program ask you to admit whom you've harmed and, when possible, make amends to them. This is to help an addict put her past where it belongs—behind her—and allow her to focus on a brighter future.

Frequently, however, family members also need help to recover. Many have acted as "enablers," unintentionally assisting and enabling an addict to pursue her addiction by excusing inexcusable behavior, by covering for her actions, and so on. They internalize guilt for the actions of the addict and their own role in that addiction and suffer stress-related problems for that time of upheaval.

As Jim, Anita's husband, said in the first interview of the book, "I remember walking into the program not knowing what caused the tightness in my chest, difficulty sleeping, tightness in my stomach, irritability, sore back, sore feet. I had to get rid of the blame, get rid of the pity, and move on. I had to begin my own recovery. I had to begin getting well— understanding that this was a disease and that I was not involved. And it was important for me to be in a group that understood."

As Jim did, family members may also need to seek help and support from others with similar experiences for their own recovery, as well as information on how to help, not unintentionally hinder, an addict's recovery. Today such help is available from groups like Co-Anon, Nar-Anon, Al-Anon and Alateen.

Co-Anon is a fledgling group, founded in 1983, to assist the family and friends of cocaine addicts. Although it's spreading the word, the group currently numbers only 45 fellowships across the nation.

Nar-Anon was founded in 1960 to provide help to the family and friends of drug abusers. Although there is no available estimate on membership, groups are located nationwide and throughout the world.

Al-Anon was founded in 1951 and lists 28,000 groups, including more than 3,000 **Alateen** groups for teenage membership, founded in 1957. Al-Anon, which counsels the family and friends of alcoholics, is located in 84 countries with 75 percent of the membership in the U.S. and Canada. Meetings are also held in prisons, hospitals, and other institutions. There is a "Lone Member Service" for persons in communities where there are, as yet, no groups.

A MINIDIRECTORY
You should be able to easily locate an anonymous program in your area through the phone book or directory assistance. If you are unable to find one in your area, however, or if you wish to obtain more information, you can contact group headquarters at the following addresses:

Cocaine Anonymous
World Services, Inc.
P.O. Box 1367
Culver City, CA 90232
(213) 559-5833

Narcotics Anonymous
World Service Office, Inc.
P.O. Box 9999
Van Nuys, CA 91409
(818) 780-3951

Alcoholics Anonymous
General Service Office
P.O. Box 459
Grand Central Station
New York, NY 10163
(212) 686-1100

Women for Sobriety, Inc.
P.O. Box 618
Quakertown, PA 18951
(215) 536-8026

Overeaters Anonymous
World Service Office
4025 Spencer St., Suite 203
Torrance, CA 90503
(213) 542-8363

Co-Anon Family Groups
P.O. Box 64742-66
Los Angeles, CA 90064
(213) 859-2206

Nar-Anon
World Service Office
P.O. Box 2562
Palos Verdes Peninsula, CA 90274
(213) 547-5800

Al-Anon/Alateen
Family Group Headquarters, Inc.
P.O. Box 862
Midtown Station
New York, NY 10018-0862
(800) 356-9996
(212) 245-3151

APPENDIX 1

The 12 Steps of Alcoholics Anonymous

Cocaine Anonymous and other anonymous groups have adapted their own versions of the original 12 Steps of Alcoholics Anonymous, which are:

1. We admitted we were powerless over alcohol, that our lives had become unmanageable.
2. Came to believe that a Power greater than ourselves could restore us to sanity.
3. Made a decision to turn our lives over to the care of God *as we understood Him.*
4. Made a searching and fearless moral inventory of ourselves.
5. Admitted to God, to ourselves, and to another human being the exact nature of our wrongs.
6. Were entirely ready to have God remove all these defects of character.
7. Humbly asked Him to remove our shortcomings.
8. Made a list of all persons we had harmed and became willing to make amends to them all.
9. Made direct amends to such people wherever possible, except when to do so would injure them or others.
10. Continued to take personal inventory, and when we were wrong, promptly admitted it.
11. Sought through prayer and meditation to improve our conscious contact with God, *as we understood Him,* praying

only for knowledge of His will for us and the power to carry
that out.

12. Having had a spiritual awakening as the result of these steps,
we tried to carry this message to alcoholics and to practice
these principles in all our affairs.

APPENDIX 2

The 12 Traditions of Alcoholics Anonymous

1. Our common welfare should come first; personal recovery depends upon A.A. unity.
2. For our group purpose there is but one ultimate authority—a loving God as He may express Himself in our group conscience. Our leaders are but trusted servants; they do not govern.
3. The only requirement for A.A. membership is a desire to stop drinking.
4. Each group should be autonomous except in matters affecting other groups or A.A. as a whole.
5. Each group has but one primary purpose—to carry its message to the alcoholic who still suffers.
6. An A.A. group ought never endorse, finance, or lend the A.A. name to any related facility or outside enterprise, lest problems of money, property, and prestige divert us from our primary purpose.
7. Every A.A. group ought to be fully self-supporting, declining outside contributions.
8. A.A. should remain forever nonprofessional, but our service centers may employ special workers.
9. A.A., as such, ought never be organized; but we may create service boards or committees directly responsible to those they serve.

10. A.A. has no opinion on outside issues; hence the A.A. name ought never be drawn into public controversy.
11. Our public relations policy is based on attraction rather than promotion; we need always maintain personal anonymity at the level of press, radio, and films.
12. Anonymity is the spiritual foundation of all our traditions, ever reminding us to place principles before personalities.

APPENDIX 3

A LIST OF THE EXPERTS:

Stephen Ambrose, clinical psychologist and director of the New Beginnings Project at the Children's Institute, Los Angeles.

Carol Atkinson, Ph.D., director of the cocaine clinic of Addiction Research and Treatment Services, University of Colorado School of Medicine.

John Barry, Ph.D., psychologist in private practice, Boston.

Sheila Blume, M.D., medical director of Alcoholism, Chemical Dependency, and Compulsive Gambling Programs at South Oaks Hospital, Amityville, New York.

Myra Byanka, founder and director of The Southwestern Behavioral Institute, Dallas.

Ira Chasnoff, M.D., assistant professor of pediatrics and psychiatry and director of the Perinatal Center for Chemical Dependence at Northwestern University Medical School, Chicago.

Blanche Frank, Ph.D., chief of epidemiology of the Bureau of Research and Evaluation for the New York State Division of Substance Abuse Services, New York City.

Elaine Johnson, Ph.D., director of the federal Office for Substance Abuse Prevention, Rockville, Maryland.

Edward Khantzian, M.D., principal psychiatrist for substance-abuse disorders at Cambridge Hospital and an associate professor of psychiatry at Harvard Medical School.

Kathleen Kinney, chairwoman of the North American Women's Commission on Alcohol and Drugs and executive director of the Lake Area Recovery Center, Ashtabula, Ohio.

Kevin McEneaney, senior vice-president and director in charge of clinical services for The Phoenix House, New York City.

Marva Miller, former addiction counselor with the now-defunct Beverly Glen Hospital cocaine program, Los Angeles.

Delores Morgan, M.D., former director of addictionology services at Mount Sinai Medical Center, Miami.

Michael Meyers, M.D., medical director of Choices at Brotman, Brotman Medical Center, Los Angeles.

William Rader, M.D., founder and clinical director of the Rader Institute, Los Angeles.

Lori Temple, psychologist at University of Nevada, Las Vegas.

Susan Thompson, former executive with a Los Angeles–based employee-assistance progam (EAP).

Michael Tinken, vice-president of community relations for Lifeline cocaine dependency treatment center, Chicago.

Arnold Washton, Ph.D., founder and executive director of the Washton Institute on Addictive Disorders, New York City.

Gloria Weissman, deputy branch chief of the Community Research Branch Division of Applied Research of the National Institute on Drug Abuse (NIDA).

ABOUT THE AUTHOR

Vicki D. Greenleaf has written for more than 30 national and inter-national publications, including *Playboy, Playgirl, Interview, US, USA Today,* the *Chicago Sun-Times,* and the *Philadelphia Inquirer. Women and Cocaine* is her first book.

Greenleaf also spent several years as a general-assignment reporter in her hometown of Lancaster, Pennsylvania. She has worked exten-sively as an entertainment writer, but today considers her area of spe-cial interest to be women's issues.

Greenleaf currently resides in Los Angeles, California, where she also serves as vice president of public relations for LIVE Entertain-ment Inc., a national distributor of entertainment software.

She is married to Julien Bohbot, is active in animal-rights issues, and has a tabby cat named Olliver.